HOW I WON THE WAR
FOR THE ALLIES

HOW I WON THE WAR
FOR THE ALLIES

One Sassy Canadian Soldier's Story

To Debbies and John

Bost wiches

Doris Gregory

Doris Gregory

RONSDALE PRESS

HOW I WON THE WAR FOR THE ALLIES
Copyright © 2014 Doris Gregory

RONSDSALE PRESS
3350 West 21st Avenue, Vancouver, B.C., Canada V6S 1G7
www.ronsdalepress.com

Layout and design: Jan Westendorp, Kato Design & Photo
Cover photo: The author swimming at Bournemouth, August 1944.
    Photo by Jeanne White.
Photo on frontispiece: Studio portrait of the author, July 1942.
Author photo (page 201): Tamara Roberts, Studio Two Photography
Editing: Naomi Pauls, Paper Trail Publishing
Paper: Ancient Forest Friendly Rolland Opaque (FSC)—100% post-consumer waste,
    totally chlorine-free and acid-free

Ronsdale Press wishes to thank the following for their support of its publishing program: the Canada Council for the Arts, the Government of Canada through the Canada Book Fund, the British Columbia Arts Council and the Province of British Columbia through the British Columbia Book Publishing Tax Credit program.

Library and Archives Canada Cataloguing in Publication

Gregory, Doris, 1921–, author
    How I won the war for the allies : one sassy Canadian
soldier's story / Doris Gregory.

Includes bibliographical references and index.
Issued in print and electronic formats.
ISBN 978-1-55380-317-1 (print)
ISBN 978-1-55380-319-5 (ebook) / ISBN 978-1-55380-318-8 (pdf)

    1. Gregory, Doris, 1921–. 2. World War, 1939–1945—Personal
narratives, Canadian. 3. Canada. Canadian Army. Canadian
Women's Army Corps—Biography. 4. Women soldiers—Canada—
Biography. 5. University of British Columbia—Students—Biography.
I. Title.

D811.G743 2014   940.54'8171   C2013-907055-9
                                              C2013-907056-7

At Ronsdale Press we are committed to protecting the environment. To this end we are working with Canopy (formerly Markets Initiative) and printers to phase out our use of paper produced from ancient rain forests. This book is one step towards that goal.

To my children, Linda, Brian, and Wayne,
my life's greatest joy

CONTENTS

Preface / ix

1   From Student to Soldier / 1
2   The Atlantic Crossing / 16
3   Introduction to London / 20
4   Hospitality in Aberdeen and Torquay / 30
5   Non-Heroes / 39
6   Army Blunders and Air Raids / 49
7   Civilians and the International Scene / 55
8   Settling into the Wartime Routine / 63
9   Highs and Lows / 70
10   The Build-Up to D-Day / 85
11   Summer Fun, Military Muddles, Buzz Bombs / 95
12   Flying Hats and Fabulous Coffee / 108
13   More Than One Kind of Wound / 116
14   Winter Chills / 128
15   Irish Spring / 136
16   Exiting Éire / 150
17   The Golden Summer / 159
18   Going Home / 174
     Notes / 181
     For Further Reading / 198
     About the Author / 200
     Index / 203

PREFACE

THIS IS A MEMOIR, dependent on memory buttressed by mementos, personal military records, and letters from overseas. Although with editorial assistance I have tried to be as accurate as possible concerning matters of historical fact, I lay no claim to absolute veracity. This is simply a record of my war as I remember it.

Originally I intended to write only for family and friends. Most have heard bits and pieces of my war story over the years, but not the complete narrative. As time went on, however, I discovered that many people had never heard of the Canadian Women's Army Corps, although most knew of our American counterpart, the WAC (Women's Army Corps). Ironically, that corps, formed almost a year after our own, modelled itself to a considerable degree upon ours. Clearly the story of the Canadian Women's Army Corps, or at least one member of it, needed to be told, in a manner which might appeal to a broader readership than that reached by official accounts or by self-published memoirs currently on the market. To this end, I have tried to take the reader into the experience with me. I want readers to feel what I felt, the positives and negatives: the camaraderie, fun, excitement, suspense as well as the tedium, worry, and occasional horror.

Throughout my story I have used the language of the time, whether or not it might be considered politically correct today. To simplify things for the reader, I have omitted last names, with only occasional exceptions. In some cases, I have changed a name in order to avoid possible distress to individuals or their families. Readers wanting more detailed information concerning army regulations, life in wartime Britain, or other relevant topics may appreciate the extensive Notes section following the story's end as well as the sources listed for further reading.

When I took on this task, I did not realize how daunting it would be. It has also, however, been a great joy. In writing this book I am indebted to so many people I could not possibly acknowledge them all. Everything I have experienced and everyone I have ever met has played a part in this production. All have helped create the person I have become. Also, I must not forget to credit my ancestors for providing a decent enough set of longevity genes. But to keep things simple, I will restrict my acknowledgements to people who have directly eased my way through life: first, my parents, who gave me unconditional love and care in those all-important early years, and later as much love and care as they were able, and my brother Gordon, my only sibling, who provided needed moral support through difficult times. I am indebted to my family too for faithfully preserving some fifty letters I sent home from overseas. Those letters provided many details otherwise forgotten.

Next, I have to thank the friends and teachers who over the years kept urging me to write. I owe a special debt to Dorothy Mawdsley, Dean of Women at the University of British Columbia, who as my high school English teacher and later at university aided and abetted my journalistic aspirations.[1] And then there are the current contributors, most notably my creative writing teacher, Ruth Kozak, whose enthusiastic support and wealth of valuable suggestions kept me slaving away at the computer for the past year or two. Without Ruth's urging I would never have attended the writers' fair where I met the genial and ingenious Ben Coles, whose suggestions added much to the final product. Of course, few writers can hope to succeed without the indispensable assistance of a first-rate editor, functioning as intellectual midwife. I count myself lucky to have had patient, long-suffering Naomi Pauls filling this role. Hers has not been an easy task, putting up with myriad last-minute changes and additions as various things floated to the surface of my memory. Her attention to detail and helpful suggestions have kept me from falling flat on my face and done much to improve the original script. I also must thank my daughter, Linda Gregory, for her excellent suggestions and careful reading of the manuscript in its later stages.

One person almost invariably remains unacknowledged by authors in sections like this. That is the book's designer, unsung hero or heroine of many a volume. Yet the presentation, especially the cover, but also the choice of fonts, paper, format, arrangement of pictures, and so on contribute greatly to the book's appeal. I'm going to break with tradition here and thank talented Jan Westendorp in print. Her creative suggestions impressed me from the start and shine through in the many details of the book's excellent design.

There is yet one more person who must be named. I offer heartfelt thanks to my publisher, Ron Hatch of Ronsdale Press, for bravely taking a chance on an unknown like me and gently prodding me to add important finishing touches to the final manuscript. Without his careful scrutiny and expertise, this book would not exist in its present form.

I owe much to all these people. However, in producing this book the final call has been mine. Any errors or flaws will have to be laid at my door. Mea culpa!

Considering my nonagenarian status, I would be remiss in failing to express my thanks to those whose tender mercies have helped me maintain excellent health and a happy mood. They include physicians, the podiatrist who keeps my flat feet happier than in army days, energetic and energizing fitness instructors, and long-term supportive caregivers. The latter have proved invaluable in relieving me of tedious chores in order that I might save my energy for more enjoyable activities, including writing.

I must not forget my army buddy, Jeanne White, fellow adventurer and photographer par excellence, responsible for the cover photo and several other images. (Also, I cannot count the number of times she has urged me to write this story.) Jeanne has published four photography books of her own, three of them during the past five years.

Finally, thanks to my children, who have provided both encouragement and motive. After all, this book began as a legacy for them and their children. Thanks also to the many friends and acquaintances who have chuckled over my war stories and urged me to put them in writing. I can't name all of you, but you know who you are. May you and all who enter here enjoy what you find.

CHAPTER ONE

FROM STUDENT TO SOLDIER

I<small>T IS EARLY</small> J<small>ANUARY</small> 1943. We have been in London two weeks. I'm walking along the Strand with two of my friends, and two Canadian soldiers who have offered to show us around and take us to their favourite pub. The street is completely dark but the night is cold and clear, perfect for us. We don't know yet that this kind of night is also perfect for enemy bombers.

The siren begins its sudden, loud, piercing up-and-down wail. The soldiers don't react. They are used to it. Besides, one of the fellows is in the midst of an intriguing story, and we all just continue walking. Then we hear the roar of approaching bombers. The noise of their engines grows louder and louder. Searchlight beams criss-cross the sky. Two beams intersect, trapping an enemy plane in brilliant light. Ack-acks (anti-aircraft guns) boom. Flak bursts and crackles all around the plane. More planes zoom overhead. The din of bombers and guns is deafening.

The few people left on the street start to run. We run, too, to the closest air-raid shelter. Not very far underground, just a basement, it offers limited protection, but at least shields us from flying debris. The shelter provides standing room only for a mix of military and civilian people, mostly the latter. We have trouble taking our eyes off one middle-aged man with a huge balloon-like growth on one side of his neck. Every few moments a bomb explodes somewhere in the distance.

"The docks," a woman says.

The man with the growth on his neck starts to sing "There'll Always Be an England" and we all join in. The atmosphere becomes quite jolly, but the air is close and we welcome the high-pitched steady note of the "all clear," heralding our escape back into the frosty air, its freshness sullied by the smell of cordite. The next day a headline in the newspaper reads "Barrage Shells Kill Twelve."

✌

People say we must have been very brave to join up. That's not the way it was, you know—not for me, at least, and I suspect not for a lot of us. Many may have been prompted by a sense of duty, especially those with boyfriends or brothers or other relatives in the forces, but I doubt we were truly brave. Brave is doing something you believe in despite being frightened to death. I, for one, was too young and giddy and foolhardy to be scared. Carefree and blessed with that conviction of invincibility common to the young, I never considered the possibility that I might not survive this incredible adventure.

Once, on the first day of the Atlantic crossing, I did experience a strange sensation in the pit of my stomach—guilt rather than fear. Two male officers had stopped me while a friend and I were walking the deck. Although our own officers had warned us against tossing anything into the sea, I had thus thoughtlessly disposed of an apple core. The two young lieutenants were very pleasant when reminding me of the rule, but I felt a pang of remorse. The feeling recurred later in the day when a couple of girls related stories of U-boat sightings. Had my tiny apple core bouncing about on the waves alerted the enemy? It took only a moment or two for me to realize the absurdity of that idea. I shrugged off the feeling and dismissed the girls' stories as unfounded rumours.

During our first lifeboat drill on the Atlantic crossing, we were warned: "If you have to jump, pull down on your life jacket or it'll come up and hit your chin and knock you out when you slam into the water!" Balancing on the sharply tilting deck, I gazed down at the cold grey sea and made up my mind. No one would last more than two minutes in that. Better to be knocked out and get it over with. Decision made, I then relaxed and enjoyed the rest of the voyage, delighting in the pitch and roll of the ship as it zigzagged its way across the U-boat-infested ocean. Only years later would we find out just how badly infested it had been. At the time of our crossing, the U-boat crisis was at its height.

People asked why I joined. I gave them the simple answer: I wanted adventure, travel, to be a part of the action. But there were other compelling reasons, which I shared with no one. I was too embarrassed. First, I needed desperately to get away from home. I had no independence, no freedom to make my own decisions, no privacy, not even a room of my own. What young woman wants to share a small bedroom with her mother, even if the relationship is a happy one? In my case, it was anything but. Although essentially a good person, extremely hard-working, well-meaning, and often generous and self-sacrificing, my mother was also extremely controlling. She loved me when I was little, but by the time I reached my teens, she became so caught up in her own emotional distress that she had little love to give. Moody and unpredictable, swinging from bursts of generosity to stinging verbal attacks, she kept Dad and me on edge. My brother, seven years my senior, was the only one permitted to stand up to her, but even he was forced to tread gently. I had to get away.

Another reason for my flight was the acute disappointment I had suffered at university. Aiming for a career in journalism, and there being no such program at the University of British Columbia (UBC), I had devoted much of my time during second year to writing for the campus newspaper, the *Ubyssey*. I worked hard, loved it, and was gratified to find many of my stories making the front page. One item, especially, caused quite a stir.

At that time, classes in second-year English at UBC were segregated by gender.[1] What made this arrangement especially unfair was the fact that the course, mandatory for all Arts students, discriminated against the female students by assigning them to teachers on the lowest rungs of the academic ladder. Second-year English was a survey course, ranging from the Elizabethan to the contemporary era. In the male-only class, the literature of each era was taught by the professor who specialized in that field. These senior professors were all male, the juniors female and/or much less experienced.[2]

I had been looking forward to the course, and so I was acutely disappointed and disgruntled during the fall term when I became aware of this situation. My fellow students, however, seemed not to even notice, except for ten girls who had a course conflict. Their problem was resolved when Dorothy Mawdsley, then Dean of Women, persuaded the two male professors involved to make an exception for them, allowing them into otherwise exclusively "male" lectures. In January, however, Professor "Freddy" Wood, teaching Victorian Drama, refused to follow suit.

A couple of girls then complained to me in my capacity as a *Ubyssey* reporter. Incensed by this additional injustice, I in turn complained bitterly to my editor, Pierre Berton.[3] "Go and crash the men's class," he urged. The next day I did so, taking the ten excluded girls and another ten female sympathizers with me. We arrived early and sat in the top row of the tiered classroom. The professor walked in, placed his notes upon the lectern, and began to speak. A few words into his first sentence, he glanced up and spotted us. He stopped abruptly. His jaw tightened. "I am not accustomed to lecturing to young women in this course." He spat the words out through clenched teeth. "Such young women will kindly vacate this room at once." A male chorus of hisses and boos followed us out.

"Freddy Wood threw us out!" I complained to Pierre.[4]

"Great! There's your story. Write it up!"

We ran it on the front page, complete with the professor's picture. I had forgotten my exact wording until more than sixty years later when a young man in the Development Department at UBC dug the article out of the archives and sent me a copy. What a diatribe! Especially the last line, which suggests that if nothing were done to appease these enraged young women, Professor Wood might "not find it safe to walk across the campus without a bodyguard." Fortunately Pierre had not given me a byline.

Today the last line of my article might warrant a charge of "uttering threats," a criminal offence, but as my daughter suggests, even had such a law existed at that time, we women might have been considered so powerless and ineffectual as to pose no threat to anyone. She's probably right.

Within hours of the paper coming out, Pierre sent me over to the professor's office to get his reaction. Professor Wood ushered me to a hard-backed chair while he settled into an easy one.

He glared at me. "I demand a retraction."

"Sir," I ventured to ask, "are you saying this event didn't occur?"

Like a seasoned politician, he avoided a direct answer. "There are very good reasons for segregated classes in second-year English."

"Sir, would you please tell me what some of them are?" I asked timidly.

"There are certain things in English literature that simply cannot be taught in mixed classes," he hissed.

I wanted to ask, "Sir, would you please tell me what some of those things are?" but restrained myself. Instead I thanked him for the interview and took my leave.

"We'll give him his retraction," Pierre told me and grinned, "but we won't have room right away." I don't remember exactly what happened to the retraction. We did consider burying some non-apology in an obscure spot on the back page, the common fate of retractions. In any case, it would not have received nearly as much attention as the original article. Canadian University Press, a news service that distributes stories from campus newspapers, had seized on my report, with the result that university newspapers all across Canada, including that at Queen's, the professor's alma mater, picked it up.[5]

That article, and others less sensational, brought me a promotion to the rank of associate editor. I thought I was on my way. The following year I would surely advance to the position of senior editor, the usual next step. Despite the fact that I was not part of the "in group" that partied together and often socialized at places like the Georgia Hotel beer parlour, I expected my hard work to pay off. Instead, the next year I was relegated to a minor role, along with the task of editing the student handbook and student directory, tedious chores no one else wanted. Pierre having graduated and gone off to war, along with a couple of other male staff members, the atmosphere at the *Ubyssey* office had changed completely. I concluded, doubtless correctly at the time, that my personality did not suit the career to which I aspired. Thus, the spring of 1942 found me at loose ends.

Almost immediately after my birthday, I went down to the old Hotel Vancouver at Georgia and Granville, newly taken over by the Army as part of Military District 11, to enlist in the Canadian Women's Army Corps. I had just turned twenty-one, minimum age for acceptance.

I had good reason for choosing the military for my escape. For almost all my young life, I had felt awkward and somewhat alienated from my peers. I didn't fit in. I was painfully self-conscious and lacking in confidence. The prospect of joining a group of young women united in a common cause, subject to the same living conditions, wearing the same uniform, appealed strongly. Perhaps there, finally, I would truly belong.

After enlisting, we didn't get into uniform or into barracks immediately. From the Hotel Vancouver, a group of us went over to Work Point, just outside Victoria, for a four-month course in typing and shorthand. We lived independently off the base and wore civilian clothes until the workmen completed our barracks and a stack of new uniforms arrived from Toronto. How proud we were of those khaki uniforms! They were beautifully tailored of fine wool barathea cloth and designed to complement almost any figure, with long, fitted, unbelted jackets and A-line skirts that swung gracefully as we marched along. We weren't the only ones to admire them, then or later. In 1944, the American military paper *Stars and Stripes* reported our uniform the winner of first prize at a London fashion show.

Alas, the uniform was more attractive than functional. The large pockets could have been useful, but we weren't allowed to put anything in them. That would have spoiled the look. The brass buttons down the front and on the pockets and the diamond-shaped badges on our lapels and hats, bearing the image of Athene, goddess of wisdom and prudent warfare, required daily polishing. Not long ago, one of my children asked about a strange piece of metal they had found among my belongings. What was it for? I had to think, for a moment.

Then I remembered all that polishing. It was a flat, U-shaped metal gadget you slid the button into, so that you could shine away without risk of sullying the uniform with polish. Well, that gleaming brass did look nice, but I doubt it helped win the war. Then, too, our satchels, their leather shoulder straps held firmly in place by epaulettes, looked great, but were too small to hold much more than a wallet and lipstick.

I was proud of the smart uniform and my new status. No longer was I simply Doris Filmer-Bennett. I had become W11508 Pte. Filmer-Bennett D.[6] It was a fresh start. I had been issued my official pay book, and I had even been issued a regulation New Testament. I enjoyed that summer at the Work Point base. My roommate, once we moved into our bright new barracks, was little Pat Dawkins, and we hit it off well. I succeeded in my clerical studies, had fun with my classmates, and dated some pleasant, though unexciting, fellows, sometimes along with Pat. The most interesting, simply because they were different, were some RAF chaps from a nearby base. They acquainted us with up-to-date British slang, like "cheesed off" (fed up), and provided first-hand accounts of the London Blitz. I loved wearing the uniform, the feeling of togetherness that came with the daily roll call and drill, the general routine. I even enjoyed the route marches. We usually sang as we marched along, songs like "Put On Your Little Khaki Bonnet,"[7] or "As We Go Marching," with lyrics written especially for us, and popular songs of the time such as "Don't Sit Under the Apple Tree" or "Over Here, Over There." In those early days of the Corps, then only a year old, the male soldiers would often quack at us as we passed by. Well, that is what we were: CWACs, pronounced "quacks." The Corps itself

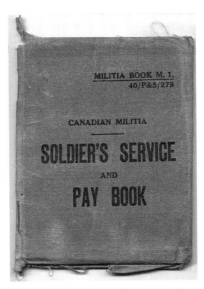

Our pay books also served
as identification and
a brief record of service.

was "the C.W.A.C.," the letters pronounced individually.

The only problem that summer had to do with my unruly mop of hair. Col. Joan Kennedy, our commanding officer, who inspected our ranks every morning, went by the book. Regulations dictated that hair must be two inches off the collar. On parade one day she ordered me to "get that hair up or have it sheared at the back." The next morning I arrived with my hair bristling with hairpins and bobby pins, but to no avail. "Go back to the hairdresser and get your hair sheared," Colonel Kennedy ordered. Had I known I would have to do that, I might have hesitated to enlist! "It's all very well for Kennedy," the girl next to me muttered after the officer had passed out

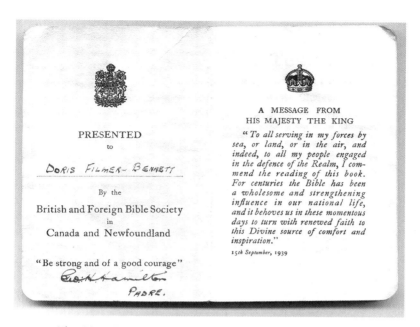

PRESENTED
to

DORIS FILMER-BENNETT

By the

British and Foreign Bible Society
in
Canada and Newfoundland

"Be strong and of a good courage"

Geo. H. Hamilton

PADRE.

A MESSAGE FROM
HIS MAJESTY THE KING

"*To all serving in my forces by
sea, or land, or in the air, and
indeed, to all my people engaged
in the defence of the Realm, I com-
mend the reading of this book.
For centuries the Bible has been
a wholesome and strengthening
influence in our national life,
and it behoves us in these momentous
days to turn with renewed faith to
this Divine source of comfort and
inspiration.*"

15th September, 1939

The New Testament signed by Padre Hamilton was
presented to us with its message from King George VI.

of earshot. "She has a neck like a swan." Happily, subsequent commanding officers were less swanlike and more sympathetic. I let my hair grow to normal length, just touching the collar. No one else ever complained.

After four months, having acquired sufficient proficiency in typing and shorthand to attain Steno status, I was posted to the military hospital in Nanaimo. That was to be my one and only interesting army job. I liked the hospital atmosphere: always something going on, people entering and leaving, every day different from the preceding one, lots of things to learn. Hospitals still fascinate me.

At that point I found my views diverging sharply from those of my associates, both male and female, on the issue of conscription.[8] Mostly I kept my opinions to myself, but my anti-conscription position grew even stronger as I observed the treatment often meted out to men who were drafted "for home defence only." They were not required at this time to go overseas. "Zombie," the derogatory term for them, was on everybody's lips but mine. Although I never personally witnessed any abuse beyond name-calling, from time to time we would hear of some of these men being set upon and severely beaten by volunteer soldiers.

One day a surgeon came into our office with an X-ray film: "Take a look at this!" Holding it up to the light, he pointed out a number of strange objects in the patient's innards. Among them I recall the metal cleat from a boot, a large nail, and what looked like a thumbtack. The patient was a conscript. The poor guy must have been desperate, resorting to such drastic measures to get out of the Army. I have no idea what eventually happened to him, but if the authorities had any sense at all, they would have discharged him on grounds of unsuitability and let him return to his farm home in Alberta. He would have been more useful to the country there.

I was no shining light in that hospital office. My first day proved a disaster. Although I had passed the clerks' course, could type fairly accurately at sixty words per minute, and was deemed to have acquired satisfactory shorthand skills, I was totally unprepared for dictation involving complicated medical terminology. I spent three hours trying to decipher what I had taken down and transform it into what I hoped was an acceptable typed report. The surgeon took one look at my gobbledegook and exploded. From Steno I was immediately demoted to Clerk-Typist, the highest trade classification I was ever to attain in the Army.

Almost every CWAC dreamed of going overseas. Since fewer than 3,000 of the more than 21,000 enlistees succeeded in realizing this dream, the vast majority had to be disappointed. Yet, given the opportunity, some did turn it down. Asked to recommend a mature, sensible girl under her command, the officer heading my unit in Nanaimo had first approached a couple of others, both of whom declined. Her third choice, and endowed with no great degree of maturity and sense, I jumped at the chance. I was thrilled at the prospect of being at the scene of the action, or some of it, and touring a country whose literature I adored and whose people included my ancestors. I immediately sent off a letter to my brother informing him of the good news.

Official envelope enclosing a letter informing
my brother of my overseas posting.

Our little MD 11 group (Military District 11 — Vancouver) joined others from Districts all across Canada at Argyle Barracks in cold, snowy Ottawa in mid-November. Lacking useful work while awaiting the call to move on, we had plenty of time to explore our nation's capital, but many long hours passed hanging out in the canteen or lounging on our bunks. Time dragged. Then came the day when big bundles arrived containing our "overseas issue" equipment. Whoever designed or selected the lingerie had little conception of what young women would want to wear. Omission of elastic in the rayon panties could be blamed on wartime shortage of rubber, but the garments need not have had such wide, droopy legs nor come in such hideous shades of brown and nauseating orange. The girdles were not only ugly, but also barely large enough for the slimmest girl to fight her way into. I can still picture Sandy, a statuesque blonde, posing in bra, girdle, and panties beside her bunk. Someone asked, "What use are these girdles?" As she groaned her way out of the contraption, she said, "I know. Chastity belts!" None of us ever wore those girdles. We stuffed them in the bottom of our duffel bags and brought them out only when required for kit inspection.

The elastic-less panties were to cause public embarrassment on more than one occasion. If the button securing them gave way during a route march or church parade, a girl had little choice but to step out of the things and keep going, hoping someone behind her would quickly scoop them up. On one occasion a stocky miss who felt her panties slipping managed to march knock-kneed long enough to pass the word down the line to the sergeant, who promptly called a halt and had the platoon form a solid phalanx around the unfortunate victim.

When the male colonel for whom the girl worked teased her the next day, she clicked her heels, saluted, and snapped, "Faulty equipment, sir!" Faulty it was, indeed.

Later on, I was to have an embarrassing experience with those panties myself, but it was my own fault. In London we could take all sorts of free City Council evening courses, and I had decided that maybe a few ballet lessons would improve my abysmal ballroom dancing skills. Since the brochure decreed that students wear shorts or very short skirts, I wore my white issue shorts with those regulation panties underneath. I rolled the droopy legs up tightly and tied them with string. Alas, that was not good enough. The ballet teacher began the first class by requiring each of us to twirl diagonally across the floor. The mere child ahead of me did it perfectly. Clumsy oaf that I was, I stumbled across by fits and starts. At the halfway point, I looked down in horror to see four inches of ghastly orange rayon hanging below my shorts. I left, never to return.

Back in Ottawa, one mid-December evening just after supper, the order came to pack. It must have been close to midnight when we clambered into army trucks for the ride to a railway siding outside of the city. A short climb in the dark up a steep bank to the tracks and at last we were on the train, bound for Halifax. The adventure was beginning in earnest. The real thrill came a couple of days later, when the train stopped and from the windows we could see a huge grey ship. Someone said, "It's the *Queen Elizabeth*! You can tell from the funnels!"

CHAPTER TWO

THE ATLANTIC CROSSING

WE GIRLS OF the Canadian Women's Army Corps, like the nursing sisters and all the other officers, were allotted sleeping accommodation in a first-class area of the ship. Housed twelve to a cabin designed for two, we slept comfortably enough in triple-decker wooden bunks. At least I did. On entry I had quickly made a dive for the bottom bunk nearest the door. Less agile than most of my companions, I was always slow at clambering up and down ladders, even on dry land, and did not fancy the prospect of having to leap down from the top bunk on a swaying ship.

Our daytime accommodation was also first-class, in a spacious converted ballroom. We thoroughly enjoyed our first day at sea. Out on the deck we mingled with soldiers from all across Canada, and in the lounge with the nursing sisters

BERTHING CARD   274

Name and Rank ....

Deck **MAIN**

Room ... **21** ...

Berth ....

PLEASE RETAIN THIS CARD

Card used for Room #21 when boarding
the *Queen Elizabeth*, December 1942.

and male officers. However, the next day all that changed. We entered the lounge to find ourselves herded behind a heavy yellow rope where our commanding officer read the riot act. She told us the colonel in charge of troops on board had said he could not risk having "those girls" destroy the morale of his men. We were forbidden all contact with the opposite sex. One girl suggested we hang a sign CONTAMINATED on the detestable rope, but of course we did no such thing. Instead we "other ranks" sat there glumly, enviably eyeing the nursing sisters, officers all, socializing with their male counterparts.

Fortunately we were free to walk the decks whenever we wished, in fact even encouraged to do so, provided we did not fraternize with male soldiers of whatever rank. I enjoyed being out on deck in any kind of weather, and what weather we had! As might be expected of the North Atlantic in December, winds blew with hurricane force and our big ship pitched and shuddered and rolled as huge waves swept over the prow. For a couple of days about a quarter of our number failed to show up at the two daily meals. Luckily I proved to be a good sailor, ate well, slept well, and delighted in the bracing sea air. I did feel sorry for those less fortunate, especially the thousands of soldiers crammed into the hold, for whom it must have been a miserable trip.

My shipboard card for the third sitting in
the dining room at Table 23.

Someone just on the other side of the rope barrier had a small gramophone or radio playing popular songs. Years later, whenever I heard the lyrics "I'm dreaming of a white Christmas" I would picture that crowded lounge, see the horizon going up and down, and almost feel the motion of the ship. At the time, however, sitting there was boring and a bit galling, watching the fun that people around our own age but of superior rank were having on the "right side" of the barrier. My gutsy friend Phyllis, five years older and a lot more assertive than most of us, was not easily put down. In an elevator one day, a nurse escorted by a male officer looked her up and down and commented haughtily, "I didn't know other ranks were permitted on the elevators," whereupon Phyllis pointed to a sign that read OFFICERS AND LADIES ONLY. "Ma'am," she said, "even though I have volunteered to serve my country, I believe I still belong in this category."

We were all of us young, with a lot of growing up to do. That nurse may well have had a lot of rough times ahead of her and ended by contributing far more to the war effort than either Phyllis or I did, although my friend did later dodge a few enemy shells and bullets over on the Continent.

Chaperoned by the sympathetic elevator operator, Phyllis and Lil and I subsequently passed the occasional half-hour parked between floors with a deck of cards and a couple of fellows Phyllis had known at home. Not very smart, if we had ever been torpedoed. But what chance would we have had anyway? We were alone, no convoy, no protection other than hopelessly small gun emplacements we could see high above the promenade deck. The *Queen* relied on speed. The largest liner then afloat, with close to seventeen thousand troops on board, what a prize she would have been for some U-boat crew! Thanks to speed and strategic charting, she eluded them all and continued ferrying troops across the Atlantic throughout the war.

CHAPTER THREE

INTRODUCTION TO LONDON

O N THE NINETEENTH of December, we sailed across the unexpectedly calm Irish Sea to the port of Greenock, Scotland. It must have taken hours to unload our ship's huge cargo of troops and transfer us all to the waiting trains, but over time my memory of that process has faded. I recall only the sight of the little British train, a mere toy compared to our Canadian giants, and the cramped compartment where six or maybe eight of us squeezed together, feet resting on kit bags. Darkness closed in too early for us to see much of the country-side we were travelling through. Lacking our usual sit-down dinner, we became desperately hungry. That was fortunate, because a corporal soon came along with K-rations, and only hunger would have made those palatable. One needed strong teeth as well, unless content to simply suck on the almost impenetrable high-protein biscuit. However, the meal proved strangely satisfying. The nutritionists and manufacturers had done their research well.

We reached London just before midnight. All was blackness, but still we could make out the shapes of buildings. Having heard so much about the Blitz of 1940–41, I was surprised to see so many edifices still standing, but then our route did not take us through the worst-hit areas. A mere half-hour after leaving the train we reached our barracks, the old Chesham Hotel, just off the Strand. A small group of girls and a couple of their officers from the first CWAC draft,[1] which had arrived about six weeks earlier, welcomed us with a good hot meal and the very British "nice cup of tea." Then we were off to bed, this time in cots rather than bunks, and only two to a room. I fell asleep immediately.

The next morning I woke a few minutes before reveille, giving me enough time to explore our new abode. My room on the second floor, shared at that time with Phyllis, was near the end of a long corridor. Next to it a bathroom housed an old-style claw-footed tub. A line of bright green paint two inches from the bottom marked the maximum allowable water height for our once-a-week bath. However, to my knowledge no one ever checked either the water height or the number of baths. Farther down the hall, another room provided toilet facilities for the probably twenty-five girls on that floor, all but one housed two to a room. The more senior NCOs (non-commissioned officers) had single rooms. So far as I recall, all four floors were identical.

This was a walk-up hotel, at least it was for us. There may have been a freight elevator somewhere. With those long corridors, and the bathroom occupying the end where one might expect to find a fire escape, that place would have been a terrible fire trap if hit by incendiary bombs. The authorities must have thought so too, for a month or two after our arrival they equipped the building with Davy belts. One evening we assembled on the fourth (top) floor for a fire drill introducing us to the use of these. After being firmly strapped into a light harness, you sat facing inward on the edge of the windowsill and pushed yourself backward until your rear end was hanging over the sill's outside edge. Then, taking a deep breath and gritting your teeth, you shoved yourself, or if hesitant were shoved, out of the window. Told not to look down, you concentrated on pushing hard with your hands and feet against the rough brick wall as the cable lowered you to the ground. It was a little scary for us all, more so for those with a greater than usual fear of heights, but refusal was unthinkable.

In the Chesham Hotel we lived more warmly than most civilians, whose homes lacked central heating. We ate better, too, though far from the way we did in Canada. The first breakfast came as a shock. Looking forward to a steaming cup of coffee, I gazed sadly at the anemic liquid dribbling out of the urn: weak tea with a little powdered milk and sugar already added. Scrambled eggs, also powdered, a fat sausage (by law no more than seventy percent breadcrumbs) and a tasteless slice of grey-coloured bread completed the meal.

Those in charge had given us a couple of days to get oriented before taking up our duties. Free to explore on our own, we set out, in twos and threes and fours. It was the week before Christmas. Never had I felt so cold. Being from Vancouver, I was used to rain and dampness, but this was different: more penetrating, knifing right through to the bone. Our heavy greatcoats, which had kept us warm while waiting "on draft" in snowy Ottawa, did not do the job here, would not until we adjusted to the climate.

Walking along the Strand towards Trafalgar Square, we gawked at buildings sliced vertically in half during the Blitz two years earlier. I felt like a voyeur, gazing up into living rooms and kitchens and bathrooms, the latter often with bathtubs and sinks intact but askew. It seemed almost sacrilegious to be staring at such intimate evidence of personal tragedy —loss not only of home and possessions but also likely of lives. Most of the rubble had long since been cleared away, but the exigencies of war could not spare personnel to raze what was left standing of the buildings.

Coming to pigeon-cluttered Trafalgar Square, we admired Nelson's column and the imposing National Gallery behind it, and off to the right, the exterior of St. Martin-in-the-Fields. We would come to know the interior during future church parades. Many of the clerks and stenos among us would grow much more familiar with Canada House, the handsome modern edifice on the other side of the square. In wartime we knew it as CMHQ, short for Canadian Military Headquarters. Thence we proceeded on to Pall Mall (pronounced "pell mell," my parents had told me), Whitehall, and over to Westminster Abbey and the Parliament Buildings and Big Ben, with its famous Westminster chimes. I had seen all this in 1932, on a short visit with my parents. Now, a decade later, a kind of drabness had settled on everything.

The next day we reported for work at our various locales. My job at CMHQ proved deadly dull, confined largely to typing out long lists of officers' names and qualifications. I wasn't a highly skilled typist, and in that era before liquid correction fluid, fixing typos was an arduous task, especially since almost everything had to be done in triplicate. I tried desperately to avoid making errors, but sometimes we were under pressure to produce the required material as quickly as possible, and at such times my error rate inevitably doubled.

There were three of us typists, who worked on machines with eighteen-inch-wide carriages. A line would start off with the officer's name, and then his regiment, regimental number, rank, age, whatever staff college courses he might have taken, and his level of performance in them. Copying from handwritten sheets, we had to be careful to place a ruler under the line we were reading, so that the qualifications would be listed against the appropriate officer's name. On one occasion, the brigadiers who met every so often to determine the future of these officers spent an hour arguing about a particular candidate, until one of them said, "I taught that course. I don't remember this fellow being in it." His memory had served him right. That course designation should have been listed against the officer next on the list.

Our colonel stormed into the office, demanding to know who had typed that particular page. No one could remember. Someone must have let the ruler slip. It could well have been me, bored as I was with the job. Worse than the work itself was the fact that it came in spurts, with frequent spells of forced idleness. The colonel banned both personal letter-writing and recreational reading. "It doesn't look right," he said. "If you want to read, you can study *KR Can*." *King's Regulations Canadian*[2] was the military Bible, the only book on hand other than the dictionary. Idleness did not seem to bother the other girls, who filled the time with chitchat—which our precious colonel did permit. I took refuge in daydreaming about the coming evening or weekend.

We loved those evenings and weekends. In London we met and mingled with military personnel from all over the world. Despite the variety, we were usually drawn more to our Canadian guys, or they to us, or maybe they tended to predominate in the places we happened upon. We seldom dated anyone in headquarters, where many of us worked. Most of those fellows were deemed unfit for the field, usually because of age but sometimes owing to some minor infirmity. Many were married, with wives back home, and/or were shacked up with English girlfriends.

And so we met our dates in the service clubs and pubs, or now and again a lad from one's hometown would come to London on leave.[3] The drawback was being unable to count on anyone. The fellow expected to arrive that week might have had his leave cancelled because of a training exercise or might have met someone more interesting. Leaves were very important, after all. You could hardly blame the guys for wanting to make the most of their break from the drudgery and tedium of camp. Life was unpredictable, but that made it more exciting. We suffered an occasional disappointment, but on the other hand we never knew when we might meet some utterly fascinating fellows.

From time to time I would hear from Ken, my ex-boyfriend from university days, a lieutenant in the Canadian Scottish Regiment. We had remained good friends, and it was nice to see him every so often when he came to London on weekend

A pamphlet listing the
"Service Clubs" in London.

leave. Quite protective of me, he was sometimes helpful in alerting me to possible dating hazards, among other things. Apart from that, Ken liked fine dining, or what passed for it in wartime London. On his visits I could always be sure of a good dinner. I remember in particular one at the Savoy, off the Strand. That was not as extravagant as it might seem today, since even the best restaurants had a cap on what they could charge for a meal, but it still felt luxurious. None of my other dates took me there.

One evening as I was coming out of the dining hall, I encountered a couple of Ken's fellow officers, vaguely familiar from university days. They were leaving a parcel for one of our sergeants. "We've brought her some nylons," one said. "She's always running out of them." I eyed the parcel suspiciously. It must have contained at least half a dozen pairs. "But we're not allowed to wear them!" I blurted out. It was true. We other ranks had to wear the unattractive lisle stockings. Only our officers were permitted the elegance of nylons, and even for them supply was strictly limited. Nylon was desperately needed for parachutes. Ken's colleagues must have acquired them through the black market.

A few days later, the irate nylon recipient grabbed my elbow and spouted out a torrent of abuse, eyes blazing. "Who the hell do you think you are, telling my officer friends I'm not allowed to wear nylons! Just take a look around here on a Saturday night and see how many CWACs are wearing nylons with their uniforms!" I was speechless.

Here was our most officious sergeant, who would get you for the slightest infraction, blatantly breaking one of the rules and defending others who did likewise. But then army life was full of inconsistencies. The sergeant broke or ignored the rules when it suited her, while coming down hard on underlings guilty of other infractions; the male officers were ready to risk their lives for their country, while undermining the system by dealing in the black market. Both illustrate the moral contradictions of the times.

I was glad I had come over with the Army rather than the Air Force. The WDs (RCAF Women's Division) lived out on their own, rather than in barracks. That meant less

GRID	MILK

R.B.12

MINISTRY OF FOOD

Name and
Initials.................................

N.R. No. or
Service No................................

Week ending

....

F.O. Stamp or
Issuing Officer

....

GRID	MILK						
		M	T	W	T	F	S	S
R.B.12 PANEL 2	**R.B.12** CHEESE						
R.B.12 PANEL I	**R.B.12** TEA						
R.B.12 QUARTER PRESERVES	**R.B.12** SUGAR						
R.B.12 EGGS	**R.B.12** BACON						
R.B.12 SPARE TWO	**R.B.12** BUTTER MARGARINE & COOKING FATS						
R.B.12 SPARE ONE	**R.B.12** MEAT						
R.B.12 POINTS **X**	**R.B.12** MEAT Detach for R.B.2						

A ration coupon

regimentation, fewer hassles from bossy non-coms like our nylon-wearing sergeant, but also many dreary chores. They had to find their own billets, do their own shopping and cart groceries home on foot and/or by bus or Underground, keeping track of currency and ration coupons. As well, they, like most civilians, often had to cope with coal fires and all the mess that entailed, or be forever feeding shillings to a tiny, rapacious gas heater. I learned later that the Army had briefly considered the same setup for us, but decided our youth and inexperience might create all sorts of difficulties, here in a big, strange city. While not oblivious to those concerns, the RCAF weighed them against the blow to morale that would follow the bombing of a barracks housing one hundred Canadian servicewomen. Having already lost several members of their headquarters staff in a direct hit in the Blitz, the Air Force High Command preferred to spread the risk.

We soon became accustomed to finding our way around London via the Underground, much easier than using the buses. The only problem was picking your way along the platform that narrowed as the evening wore on, half its width taken up with families bedded down for the night. They would get little sleep until the trains stopped running at two o'clock in the morning. Londoners told us many of these families were refugees from Malta, still traumatized from the terrific bombardment they had experienced there.

We also soon became accustomed to the blackout. Air-raid wardens constantly patrolled the streets, watching for any little cracks of light emanating from homes or pubs or other establishments. Periodically you would see a sudden shaft of light as someone entered or left a pub or restaurant. After the damp dreariness of the street, lit only by Xs scratched into black paint covering lights at intersection islands, we welcomed the warmth and conviviality of the pub. The air was inevitably stuffy, dominated by cigarette smoke and ale fumes, often combined with the dank odour of wet clothing, but that didn't bother us in the least.

We came to associate the pub with happy times. Heartily disliking the bitter taste of beer, at first I would simply sip a sherry all evening, until finally my CWAC friends objected. They argued that guys would never come over and talk to us if they saw us with expensive drinks. I compromised by ordering shandies—ale diluted with lime, lemon, or fizzy orange drink—still not to my taste but at least tolerable. The pubs were usually packed with young people, men mostly in uniform, Canadians and Brits, chatting and laughing and often breaking into some wartime song or other—songs seldom heard now, like the wistful "When the Lights Go On Again" or the raucous "I've Got Sixpence."

CHAPTER FOUR

HOSPITALITY IN
ABERDEEN AND TORQUAY

IN FEBRUARY our first leave came due. From now on, we would be getting nine days' leave every three months. Having booked a home stay through the auspices of the Sally Ann (Salvation Army), Lil and I took the long train ride to Aberdeen. "Let's go to the Highlands," I had suggested. No one had warned us how cold that area would be in midwinter. We soon found out, as we pushed against the icy North Sea wind on our way to the home of the Misses McPherson, two kind elderly spinsters who, like so many in the U.K., had generously opened their home to servicemen and women from abroad.

Their stone cottage was small and dark, but "small" meant warm and cozy, at least in the main rooms. Upstairs in our unheated bedroom we shivered and longed for our centrally heated London quarters. We undressed in one minute flat, stowing all our clothes under the covers with us, a practice we would resort to many times in the future.

The ration coupons issued with our leave passes ensured that our hostesses would not have to use any of their own few coupons on our behalf. The McPherson sisters fed us well. What the meals lacked in meat and sweets, they made up for with that home-cooked quality never equalled by army cooks preparing food for hundreds.

A torn ration coupon issued
when we were on leave.

Aberdeen was monochromatic: grey stone shops, homes, bridges, all under a slate-grey sky. One day we visited the grey-granite University of Aberdeen. Wandering into the Great Hall at the end of a lecture, we joined a line of autograph seekers. Until the gracious lady signed her name, we had no idea of her identity. I was pleased to acquire the autograph of Lady Isobel Cripps, wife of Sir Stafford Cripps, a Labour MP.

On our last day, walking down a side street, a postman following behind chatted away to us for almost a block. We understood not a word. At the corner, as we turned to go our separate ways, he came level with us, uttered a few more incomprehensible phrases, and then laughed heartily at our bewildered expressions. "Aye, lassies," he chuckled, "I was just talking the broadest Scots I know!"

"Not Gaelic?" I queried, at which he laughed still more heartily.

"Nae," said he, "just broad Scots!" As far as we were concerned, it could have been Greek.

The Misses McPherson enjoyed our report of the encounter. I think they liked us, but found us a bit brash. They were probably not used to young women. The elder one took me to task one evening regarding my alleged use of eyeshadow. I had always heartily disliked the natural bluish tinge of my eyelids and the area below my eyes. In no way would I have accentuated it by using eyeshadow, but I doubt she believed my protestations.

Another time we got into a discussion about the English. Our hostesses had no love for the "Sassenachs" south of the Border. They considered them arrogant, shallow, unreliable, and thoroughly dishonest. We were surprised and amused. There was a war on, after all, and it was not supposed to be a war between Scotland and England! The incident brought to mind a story my English-born father had once told me about seeking employment in Vancouver in the early part of the twentieth century, when Help Wanted advertisements by Scottish-owned companies ended with the warning "No Englishman need apply." There must have been exceptions to that general rule, however, since my father worked for many years as an accountant for the Brackman-Kerr Milling Company. Mr. Kerr's Scottish brogue was as thick as they come.

London was proving endlessly fascinating. Every time you walked through Piccadilly Circus or down Oxford Street or the Strand, you saw something new, something you had missed before. I was pleasantly surprised, too, at the extent of theatrical offerings, with tickets well within even our price range, some as low as one shilling sixpence. Many of us became regular attendees at the Haymarket, Leicester Square, Wyndham's, and other West End theatres. I remember seeing some wonderful performances by stars such as Alfred Lunt and his wife Lynn Fontanne, Laurence Olivier and Vivien Leigh, and plays such as *Hamlet, Arsenic and Old Lace,* and *The Doctor's Dilemma,* by George Bernard Shaw. I still have some of the programs and marvel at the low price on the cover.

More remarkable than the price is the expressed determination that London life proceed as normally as possible. Almost all include an announcement permitting members of the audience to leave should an air raid occur, but encouraging them to remain in the theatre. Never was the motto "The show must go on" more strictly adhered to than in wartime London.[1]

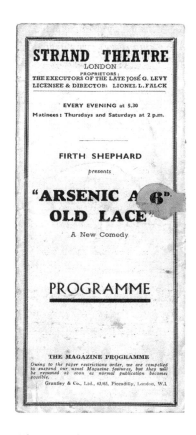

Theatre playbill advertising a very early production of Joseph Kesselring's *Arsenic and Old Lace.*

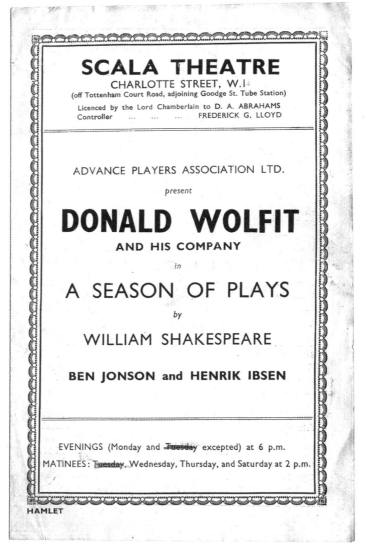

SCALA THEATRE

CHARLOTTE STREET, W.I

(off Tottenham Court Road, adjoining Goodge St. Tube Station)

Licenced by the Lord Chamberlain to D. A. ABRAHAMS
Controller   ...   .   FREDERICK G. LLOYD

ADVANCE PLAYERS ASSOCIATION LTD.

present

DONALD WOLFIT

AND HIS COMPANY

in

A SEASON OF PLAYS

by

WILLIAM SHAKESPEARE

BEN JONSON and HENRIK IBSEN

EVENINGS (Monday and ~~Tuesday~~ excepted) at 6 p.m.

MATINEES: ~~Tuesday~~, Wednesday, Thursday, and Saturday at 2 p.m.

HAMLET

Theatre playbill featuring productions of
Shakespeare, Jonson and Ibsen.

We ate out on our own only now and then. Although there was a cap on what restaurants could charge for meals, our pay schedule necessitated careful budgeting. Favourite eating spots were the Lyons Corner Houses, with their relatively inexpensive though unexciting salad bars, which always included the nutritious rollmops (pickled herring). On weekend afternoons they sometimes had a string trio in the background playing light classical music. We kept these splurges to a minimum, however, preferring to save our pennies for leave time. While mostly availing ourselves of the free lodging provided by kind Britishers, we liked now and again to stay in a hotel or hostel. Also, we always needed money for train tickets for weekend excursions. Railway passes were issued only for those on leave or on military errands.

My next such leave, in May, was a welcome break from army routine, and feisty Phyllis the ideal companion. The best weather in the British Isles was and still is to be found in the West Country: Devon and Cornwall. With this in mind, Phyllis and I booked our early May leave with a hospitable family in Torquay. The weather didn't let us down. It was glorious —sunny and often shirtsleeve warm. Our hosts, the Colmans, and their elegant home were all we could have wished for as well. Years later I was to discover we had been hosted by a branch of the prolific and prominent Colman's Mustard family.

We didn't spend a great deal of time with our hosts, however, so eager were we to explore areas of Devon and Cornwall we had read about. Both avid readers all our young lives, we longed to visit Lorna Doone country, tour Dartmoor and the rugged coastline, see Plymouth and the site where Sir Francis Drake bowled before setting sail to defeat the Spanish Armada, maybe even get to the St. Ives of nursery-rhyme fame. When we mentioned Dartmoor, the Colmans responded immediately and generously, almost in unison: "You can borrow our bicycles. It's not that far, if you don't mind a few hills."

Around noon that first day we came to what looked like a major intersection and stopped to check the large and very detailed map our hosts had lent us. We would have been lost without it, since the road signs, removed when invasion seemed imminent, had not yet been replaced. High on a windswept hill we laid our map out in the middle of the crossroads and pored over it while eating the box lunch Mrs. Colman had provided. No need to worry about traffic. We hadn't seen a vehicle since half an hour out of Torquay.

A distant, muffled crump-crump of bombs, somewhere along the coast to the east, punctuated the silence of the moors. Vast stretches of empty, almost treeless moorland extended to the horizon in all directions. Sitting there under a cloudless sky, warmed by the welcome sun, we felt at peace. The bombing was a long way off.

After considerable deliberation, we set off again, thinking to circle back to Torquay by a different route. Two hours later, over mugs of cider at a roadside pub, we discovered how wrong we'd been. We were heading for Plymouth, not Torquay! Well, we had wanted to see Plymouth anyway, no harm done. But, of course, we had to call our hosts to ask whether they minded if we extended our trip one more day. Mrs. Colman said not to worry; she was happy we were having such a good time.

As the afternoon wore on, still sunny and warm, Phyllis and I grew thirstier and thirstier. Happily, pubs became more and more frequent. We found Devon cider most refreshing. However, not until our borrowed bicycles became increasingly difficult to steer did we begin to suspect that this wasn't at all the kind of cider we had known at home. And not until one pub host queried, "Sweet or rough?" did it dawn on us that in this part of the world there were two kinds of cider. From then on, we stuck to "Sweet!"

After our day in an idyllic countryside, Plymouth horrified us. As we rode in, all was quiet as in the country, but this was an eerie silence. We pedalled past flattened block after flattened block, where once had stood houses and shops. The area had been completely razed, scarcely a stick or stone left standing. With the rubble cleared away, just crumbs of concrete littered the ground. What a pounding Plymouth must have taken sometime over the preceding couple of years.

We found lodging in a five-storey hotel, standing all by itself close to the sea, near the east bank of the Tamar River. Not fancy. But we happily settled for comfortable. We slept well. After such a strenuous day we would likely have slept well even in a haystack.

The next morning the hotel owner told us the river marked the border between Devon and Cornwall. And so we phoned the Colmans once again to see if they minded us delaying our return yet another day. One day became two, since we were to venture a considerable distance into Cornwall. We didn't get as far as St. Ives, but did happen upon another spot familiar from poetry readings, the Well of St. Keyne. Legend has it that whoever drinks first from this well, wife or husband, will be the boss. We drank deeply, not through any belief in the legend, but from sheer thirst and newly gained awareness that water from whatever source quenched thirst more effectively than cider, rough or sweet. Besides, water was cheaper.

Another night at our little hotel by the Tamar and most of a day meandering along the picturesque south coast brought us back to Torquay and the Colmans'. Rather than taking offence at our wanderings, our hostess expressed guilt at holding our ration coupons and tried unsuccessfully to give them back! Mrs. Colman then decided the least she could do was to put some of our rations and their own together and make us some Devonshire cream. She was indeed a gracious lady.

I'm ashamed to say that not until years later did it occur to me how thoughtless we had been in hanging onto the bicycles for such a long time. We had deprived our hosts of what must have been their usual means of getting around town. They would not have been in the habit of using the car, for petrol was in very short supply.

CHAPTER FIVE

NON-HEROES

UNLIKE MOST of my confreres, I had come into the Army from the intellectually stimulating atmosphere of university rather than a humdrum office or retail job. I wasn't used to boredom and hated it. I could hardly wait to escape into the freedom of evenings and weekends and leaves.

Shortly before that leave in the West Country, my pleas for a more interesting job had led to a change of both workplace and barracks. Unfortunately, the new job, while certainly more challenging than the last, involved a great deal of statistical work and the use of a big, heavy, aging calculating machine that kept breaking down. When it broke down, it would emit a horrible buzzing noise until unplugged. I would have to wait for Major Ferguson, my supervisor and a University of Edinburgh trained statistician, to get it running again. Since for unknown reasons he was sometimes out of the office for a full or half day, I spent considerable time doing very little.

I don't know if the project he had me working on just came to an end or he merely became impatient with my lack of mechanical aptitude. In any case, after three or four months he asked me to go out into the main office and "help with the filing for a week or two." That meant filing Q (qualification) cards[1] by regimental numbers, the most soul-destroying task imaginable. Day after day, hour upon hour, I pulled out stacks of large cards according to a list of numbers and put away other stacks. The work was not only deadly dull but also physically tiring, as the file cabinets were heavy wooden brutes, with drawers that did not easily slide in and out. The "week or two" stretched into months. My complaints to the medical officer about aching feet had liberated me from the occasional half-hour of church-parade marching, but not from the daily seven or eight hours of standing required by this job. That made no sense. Army decrees often failed to make sense, but I had expected better from the Selection of Personnel Office.

Working in the Records Building, and particularly with the Q cards, did have one redeeming feature: access to a wealth of personal information on every male soldier in the Canadian Army below officer rank. I made good use of this access, both on my own account and occasionally for the benefit of fellow CWACs. Nothing was labelled TOP SECRET or even SECRET. The Q cards certainly should have been stamped CONFIDENTIAL, but I don't remember that they were. No one in the department ever said anything to me about confidentiality. I passed data along to CWAC friends only when crucial for their protection, as for instance when a friend's date failed to disclose his married state,[2] but I had absolutely no qualms about seeking out the smallest detail for myself.

The Records Building was a gossipy place. Most of the female employees were civilians, already installed in their jobs well before we few CWACs arrived. They had known most of the male officers and NCOs for a long time. Some of these women were living with one, dating one on a regular basis, or perhaps hoping to do one or the other. Thus many stories circulated around the building. I heard a few over lunch in the canteen, enough to make me wonder if field units sent their misfits up to headquarters because they could do less damage there. Was that really so?

I recall one of our Selection of Personnel majors in whose case it probably was. The story went that he had returned to his field unit one night very drunk. When the sentry demanded, "Who goes there?" the major fired at him. Fortunately the

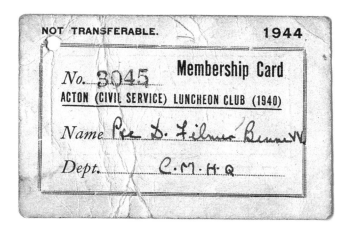

My canteen card entitled me to free food of
uncertain quality, accompanied by plenty of gossip.

major was a poor shot. This particular story rang true for me because of a subsequent event.

Following the Saturday wedding of one of our civilian stenographers, the major in question suddenly disappeared, without explanation. On Monday he was no longer in his office. By Wednesday his desk had been emptied. The bride later told us what had happened at the wedding reception. In a drunken rage the officer was alleged to have thrown a waiter through a plate-glass window. Later on, a rumour circulated that he had been court-martialled, sent back to Canada, and demoted to the rank of corporal. I hadn't had much to do with this character. All I recall is a very shiny bald head and unsmiling, grumpy face. However, he was much disliked in the department. The rumour about his ultimate fate may have merely reflected what his staff and co-workers wished had happened.

I was not supposed to have access to officers' files, but once I happened upon a stack of them, including one bearing the name of the handsome English teacher I once had a crush on in high school. It gave interesting hints about his love life. Apparently some of our personnel officers liked to play psychiatrist and inquire into sexual matters. Another time, when a pile of letters had been carelessly left on a desk, I took advantage of the empty office during lunch break to peruse them, including one which certainly should have been stamped CONFIDENTIAL. It concerned a captain newly arrived to head up another department in the building, giving some vague comments about his behaviour in the field. The letter was carefully worded, almost cryptic in style, and I didn't quite know what to make of it.

A few months later Ken told me a story that appeared to

clarify the situation. At that fellow's field unit, the officers' mess was in a lovely old manor house with a portico above the main entrance. One evening during a dance, the officer in question, in a hurry to relieve himself, had reportedly let fly from this lofty height at the very moment when the brigadier was passing below.

Sometimes, to relieve the boredom, I took time out from filing to browse the files. Soldiers' answers to the question "Why did you join the Army?" varied widely. Most had responded with the standard "To serve my country" or words to that effect, but others answered "To get away from my wife," "To get three square meals a day," "To see the world," "To have a helluva good time," and so on.

Indeed, not all of the men who rushed to enlist as soon as war began were inspired by patriotism. This is not to take away from the many fine men who were, but Canada was just coming out of the Depression, and many enlistees were either unemployed or working at menial jobs and eager for change. As one military policeman I briefly dated pointed out to me, the Army might have looked pretty good to a man recently out of prison, jobless and penniless. Decades later, a veteran told me of a conversation he'd had with a fellow recruit in the fall of '39. The man said, "I know I've seen you before. Where was it? Was it up in Yellowknife? Newfoundland? Saskatoon? Oh, I know! It was KP, wasn't it?" My acquaintance didn't know what he was talking about. KP? And then another soldier sitting nearby burst out laughing. KP, as any self-respecting Canadian felon would have known, stood for Kingston Penitentiary.

I later met one far from heroic character. According to his own account, he had to get out of town in a hurry because he had gotten one of his girlfriends pregnant. In a panic he dashed off to the recruiting office. By late January 1940, he was safely far beyond reach, not only out of the town, but also out of the country, sent with the First Canadian Division to a location near the old military town of Aldershot in southern England.

Weather that January was particularly foul—bitterly cold, with incessant rain. Temporarily housed in tents hastily set up in a muddy field, lining up outside the mess tent for their meals, enduring daily route marches and drills, the men of this fellow's unit were miserable. One day, after a particularly gruelling five-mile run with full pack in the never-ending rain, our non-hero arrived back at his leaky tent to find mail from his hometown. Eagerly he tore open the slightly soggy envelope to find a belated Christmas card from the former girlfriend. On it she had scrawled a short note: "It turned out to be a false alarm, I wasn't pregnant after all! Hope you're enjoying Army life!" It couldn't have happened to a more deserving guy.

⁓

The men I met during most of that first year in England varied from horrible to tolerable to pleasant-but-unremarkable through somewhat interesting to really-interesting-but-never-to-be-seen-again. In the latter category were some very pleasant American officers who entertained us one weekend in the quaint little village of Bury St. Edmonds. One of our girls had taken three of us with her when she went to visit her fiancé, whose air base was nearby. He and his three friends invited us to their mess for a scrumptious dinner and a movie Saturday night, escorted us back to our hotel, and came up to our room for drinks. The next day they drove us around the countryside in a jeep before seeing us off on the train. They were great company and thorough gentlemen. Unfortunately, except for our affianced friend, who married her beau a few months later, none of us saw any of them again. Oh well, you win some, you lose some.

I remember only two men in the truly horrible category. One I couldn't get out of my mind for a long time. He lurched across the pub floor, flushed and bleary-eyed, rumpled blue tunic half unbuttoned and tie askew, to plop into the unfortunately vacant chair next to mine. He reeked of alcohol and leaned uncomfortably close. Almost immediately he launched into a tirade denouncing a "cowardly" fellow pilot who, unable to find the target, had just dumped his bombs in the Channel and flown back to base. "Wasted good bombs. Could've dropped them on a school or hospital. Like me, last load. School, direct hit!" His story didn't quite ring true for several reasons, but it nevertheless made my blood run cold. That one of our Canadian pilots would say such things horrified me. I didn't consider at the time what this lad might have suffered, how many of his friends he had seen shot down, what horrors he had witnessed. I felt only disgust.

Not long after, I read a newspaper item that disgusted me still more, since it recounted something that had happened only the day before and the reporter was endorsing the action taken. A German plane had been shot down in a Surrey field. As the badly wounded pilot was trying to crawl away from the burning plane, the farmer came out with a pitchfork and tossed him back into the flames. The report ended with the warning: "That's what the enemy can expect from our brave British people."

I have read a number of memoirs written by Canadian women who served overseas in World War II. Among the best is that of Nano Pennefather-McConnell, an RCAF WD (Women's Division) sergeant who served in London during the same period I did, although we were to meet only decades later. In her memoir she mentions a conversation she and a friend had on a London street with a couple of Canadian infantry lieutenants. The young women asked them, "What about prisoners?" Nano reports that the men looked at each other and then one said flatly, "We don't take prisoners."

We want to believe that only our enemies commit atrocities. We hate to think of anyone on our side capable of doing terrible things. Equally, we sometimes find it difficult to imagine anyone on the other side capable of compassion. I admit I was a little surprised to read, in *Old Stones*, a poignant family memoir by the Canadian author Anthea Penne, about the medical care provided in enemy territory for her father, an RCAF pilot shot down over Normandy a few weeks after D-Day. True, the farmer and his son who rescued him at the risk of their own lives were French, not German. However, when a French doctor they called found the wounds so bad that the pilot needed hospital care and they therefore had to contact the German authorities, the farmer and his son suffered no adverse consequences and the pilot reports having been treated well by the Gestapo.

The hospital, being a POW institution presumably hastily set up, provided pretty rough care, with a lack of anesthesia for surgery, confinement in cells rather than hospital wards, and a meagre diet. It was hardly ideal, but unlike the German pilot who was forked back into the flames in Britain, Anthea's father lived to tell the tale. Nevertheless, since the amputation was later considered poorly done, and the American Negro[3] regiment that liberated the hospital a month or two later found the patients malnourished, it may have been only this early liberation that saved the lives of Anthea's father and other prisoner-patients.

Another fellow in the "horrible" category—to my mind worse than the drunken pilot—was an American master sergeant who had arranged to meet me at CMHQ after work and take me to dine at the Charing Cross Hotel, not far from my barracks off the Strand. We had just finished the main course when he told me about a tea dance he'd gone to that afternoon. "There was this pretty blonde English girl dancing with a big buck nigger," he said. "So 'course I went over and tapped him on the shoulder. He'd got the nerve to tell me this wasn't a tag dance. I said, 'I'm from the South, boy! Move!' You should've seen him go!"

Well, I thought to myself, *you* are going to see *me* go! But not just yet. "That's disgusting," I told him. "That's a terrible way to treat a fellow soldier, a terrible way to treat any human being. You ought to be ashamed of yourself."

"They're not human beings. They're just animals!" he shot back. "Do you want me to walk out of here right now?"

Oh no, I thought. *You* are not going to walk out on *me*, I am going to walk out on *you*, but only after I've had dessert! And so I changed the subject abruptly: "Look at that uniform over there. I've never seen one like it. What on earth is it?" Actually, I did know it was that of the Free French, but he didn't. I can't remember what I had for dessert, but immediately after finishing it I excused myself to go to the loo and slipped down a hallway to the exit. Happily I never saw that bigot again.

CHAPTER SIX

ARMY BLUNDERS AND AIR RAIDS

M^{Y COMPLAINTS} to the medical officer finally got me off my feet into a sedentary and slightly more interest-ing but still totally unchallenging job, copying information by hand from one set of cards onto another. Little did I know then that my complaints about aching feet would pay off sixty years later. Captain Brown, bless his heart, had carefully entered them into my medical records, providing invaluable support in qualifying me for disabled veteran's status. The pen-sion itself is minuscule, but brings with it a number of other welcome benefits.

While the job proved disappointing, and I had to take a bus or the Underground to work, the quarters to which I was moved because of the job change were definitely a step up. The six new-looking, centrally heated houses stood just a block from

Lancaster Gate tube station, close to Hyde Park.[1] Six, sometimes seven, of us shared what had probably been intended as
the master bedroom, with en suite bathroom, on the second
floor. I still remember the address: 13 Stanhope Terrace. In
1987, I revisited it. The formerly straight road now curved as it
passed Sussex Square, which we abutted, but except for a fan-
cier front door, the exterior of "my" house looked the same as
ever. It still looked like new. I probably couldn't afford to live
there now.

Every fourth or fifth weekend we were supposed to put in
several hours at the switchboard in the administration building across the square. That must once have been an impressive home, with a huge entry hall and side staircases at right
and left curving down from the mezzanine above. Never
well-coordinated at the best of times, I dreaded coping with
the switchboard, inevitably getting the cords tangled up and
incurring the wrath of many a girl inadvertently cut off in the
middle of a conversation with her boyfriend. I did my best,
but after I had cut off a couple of our officers' calls, my name
mysteriously disappeared from the roster and I went back to
enjoying mostly duty-free weekends.

About eleven o'clock one Sunday morning, two of my roommates and I looked out the window to see four policemen, one
at each corner of the intersection. A girl came running in to
tell us the Royal Family would be passing in a few minutes
on their way from Paddington Station to Buckingham Palace.
We rushed down, stationing ourselves at the curb to salute as
King George VI, Queen Elizabeth (later to be known as the
Queen Mother), and the two young princesses, Elizabeth and

Margaret Rose, drove by. There must have been more than one vehicle, but I can remember only one. At any rate, we were alone on the curb and the royal smiles and waves were solely for us. We were thrilled.

Sometime in the winter of 1943–44, we experienced a series of air raids over a relatively short period, maybe three or four months. Our commanding officer, acting under directives from her superiors in London High Command, ordered rope-climbing apparatus to be installed on the top (third) floor of each of our half-dozen houses. A heavy rope attached to a stanchion firmly bolted to the wall lay coiled on the floor, below a hall window. Before we received any orders, girls working in the orderly room had spread the story. We all knew we would be ordered to climb down that rope to the pavement below. In my house everyone was terrified. We were even more alarmed when we inspected the rope and discovered how far apart the knots were. Clearly those were climbing ropes for men, not women. Some of our girls stood little more than five feet tall.

At my former barracks, the old Chesham Hotel, I had descended four storeys, but in a secure Davy belt harness. Along with several others I decided to disobey current orders and face punishment, however severe, rather than risk falling forty feet onto the pavement. Our cook, an older, very robust and determined woman, yanked at the stanchion until it came loose, rendering it unusable and doing considerable damage to the plaster wall in the process. "That's that," she announced. "Now they can't make us go down *this* rope." As it happened, the officers started with one of the other houses. The first girl ordered out fell halfway down. Our commanding officer abruptly cancelled the exercise. The poor girl spent several weeks in hospital and six months later was still limping, apparently from a fractured heel bone that had not healed properly.

As per regulations, a formal Court of Inquiry was held. Not surprisingly, the only people present were our own officers, who themselves would have been acting only under orders from above. If any repercussions followed, the news never filtered down to us. No one ever questioned us about the damage to the wall, either.

At CMHQ a few heads must have, or should have, rolled over the incident. One of our young women could easily have been killed. Whoever authorized the exercise had to be at least a captain, more likely a major or colonel. One might well ask how anyone so stupid could have managed to attain that rank. However, considering one or two other equally stupid though less potentially dangerous decisions I saw made by CMHQ officers, common sense and a reasonable intelligence level were not always necessary requirements for promotion. Perhaps Groucho Marx wasn't entirely wrong in saying, "Military intelligence is a contradiction in terms."[2]

One evening Dot burst into the room, face ashen, tears streaming down her cheeks: "I just heard, the Free French barracks, last night, a direct hit. Seven hundred casualties!" We froze.

We lived two blocks from Hyde Park. The Free French were near it on the opposite side. Not close, considering the size of the park, but in a straight line from us.

"Are you sure?" Holly asked.

"I heard two officers talking about it."

Thus, orders posted the next day surprised no one: "Directly the Alert sounds, all members of this Company shall immediately take shelter in the basement of their respective houses, and remain there until the sound of the All Clear."

I must have been an extraordinarily deep sleeper in those days, because time after time I would wake, not to the sound of the siren or my roommates' exhortations, but only to the covers being pulled off and someone yanking me out of bed. Only then would I feel the house shaking violently from the vibrations set off by the ack-acks nearby in Hyde Park and hear the deafening boom of guns and roar of bombers overhead. I wasn't scared, just annoyed at being woken up. Even down in the basement, listening to the bombardment, I didn't feel frightened. I did experience a rush of adrenalin. Here was I, at the scene of the action, where history was being made. Wow!

Only once during my entire time in London did I see someone go into hysterics during a raid. It happened down in our basement shelter. The girl, recently arrived overseas, seemed very young, probably one of those who had lied about her age on enlistment. The sergeant's quick slap on the face calmed or at least quieted her. At the time, I'm afraid I reacted with acute embarrassment rather than sympathy.[3]

One night my friend Jeanne and I were ordered to stand fire-watch duty. At the sound of the alert, we posted ourselves just outside our front door, with shovels and buckets of sand, watching for any stray incendiary bombs. We stood there listening to the roar of enemy planes as they zoomed towards us, their ominous roar accompanied by the ear-splitting din of our anti-aircraft batteries. We could see the planes overhead, lit up by searchlights, and the crackling bursts of flak from our anti-aircraft fire, but this time we heard few bombs drop. This was primarily an incendiary raid, and incendiaries make less noise. None fell close, but some came down a few blocks away.

With the steady note of the All Clear, we broke the rules and walked over to where flames were shooting up. An air-raid warden was struggling to help three firemen with the hoses, pouring a steady stream of water on the blaze. Occupants of the burning home and the threatened adjacent ones huddled together on the sidewalk with their blankets and a few hastily gathered precious items. Powerless to help, Jeanne and I left quickly. It seemed cruel to stand there watching this disaster.

CHAPTER SEVEN

CIVILIANS AND THE INTERNATIONAL SCENE

Having taken a number of thought-provoking courses during my years at UBC, I was greatly interested in exchanging ideas on politics and social customs with the civilians I met both during the course of my work and in the pubs. This is evident in my letters home early in 1943. During my years overseas I would write many, especially to my brother, Gordon, who as a member of Canada's meteorological service was stationed in lonely outposts like Moosonee near James Bay, and Sable Island, far out in the Atlantic. Letters meant a lot to him. My early ones amuse me now, because of the way my youth and inexperience come through in them.

One dated January 17, 1943, is a good example. I had been in England less than a month, and here I was generalizing like mad and talking as though I were an authority on public opinion. I wrote: "It's amazing how often you hear civilians express the view that, after Germany is thoroughly squashed, we've got Russia to face. That view seems much more widely spread in this country than in Canada. Most Canadians I've spoken to about it toss it aside as almost an absurdity. English people, being closer to the heart of things, I suppose, feel that the danger of Russian aggression is a very real thing." Later in the same letter I comment on a conversation with a young New Zealander. I quote him as saying, "There is no room in this world for class distinctions of any kind, either the Russian or the British variety, and it is up to America to set an example to Europe by keeping straight along a middle course." I also mention my horror when this man referred to himself and to me as "colonials," a term sometimes also used by the English.

In early February I had an interesting encounter, which could have provided an opportunity for fascinating discussion. Unfortunately, I muffed it. I had met a real live suffragette, one of those brave women who suffered ridicule and often imprisonment before the First World War for their determined fight for the vote. Having read at length about some of these women, I felt truly honoured to be in the presence of one. That was all thanks to Derek Pethick, a U B C friend of my brother. Derek had given me the London address of his aunt, Mrs. Pethick-Lawrence. When I telephoned her, she immediately invited me to tea at her apartment, where I also met her niece and another younger woman, both probably in their early forties.

Emmeline Pethick-Lawrence would have been seventy-six at that time, but looked at least ten years younger. Her face was unlined and she had no sign of grey hair. How I wish now that I had done my homework and realized what an incredible woman I had the honour of meeting. I could have asked more intelligent questions and contributed more to the conversation. I'm sure she would have been interested in my attempt to strike a blow, feeble though it was, against UBC's policy of discrimination against women. Alas, at that point I was still painfully self-conscious, especially in the company of older, highly articulate individuals. Intimidated, I sat there tongue-tied. The younger women peppered me with questions about the romance in my life, at that particular point non-existent. Too bad I wasn't sharp enough to make up some titillating tales! Instead I left feeling I had been a total disappointment to them all.

Recently I have researched the life of my distinguished hostess. She was indeed a remarkable woman, in my opinion almost as remarkable as the leader of the suffragettes, Emmeline Pankhurst. That is the name we think of in connection with the movement, but Emmeline Pethick-Lawrence and her husband Frederick contributed a great deal in terms of money as well as time and effort. They also endured much hardship, including lengthy imprisonment and forced feeding when they both went on a hunger strike. Emmeline, a rebel from her early school days, when she was accused of "corrupting the other students," became a socialist after voluntary social work for a Methodist mission exposed her to the sufferings of the very poor.

So ardent a socialist was she that she refused to marry the wealthy lawyer Frederick Pethick unless he also converted to socialism. Not only did he do that, he also accepted her suggestion that on marrying they should combine their surnames, adopting the name "Pethick-Lawrence." They appear to have been absolutely devoted to each other throughout their marriage. I was happy to read that in 1945 he was elevated to the peerage and she became Lady Pethick-Lawrence, although I doubt that titles were of much importance to either of them.

I think it was in October of 1943 that Jeanne and I attended a Communist rally held on a weekend afternoon in some small and probably seldom-used theatre. True to British adherence to freedom of speech, people were at liberty to express even unpopular opinions, so long, I suppose, as they did not advocate overthrow of the government. Besides, at that time the Russians were our allies. This rally's slogan was "Second Front Now!" Well, they would have to wait a while yet.

It must have been around that time that we went to another kind of rally, or conference. At the Netherlands Club, Jeanne had met an interesting English woman by the name of Mrs. Young, who had entertained her in her home on several occasions prior to inviting the two of us to a conference of the World Unity Society. I had not previously heard of that organization nor have I since, but the people attending seemed quite distinguished, except for Jeanne and me. I don't remember much of the chairman's speech, or indeed of the discussion that followed, although it became very animated. However, I will never forget the ferocity of the argument between an Arab on one side of the room and a Jew on the other. I can still picture the scene, in that second-floor assembly room overlooking Leicester Square. Both men were gesticulating wildly and shouting at each other, talking over each other, neither listening to a word the other was saying. The rest of us sat dumbfounded, unable to make out the words of either. An American diplomat beside me turned and asked, despairingly, "How can we ever hope for real peace?"[1]

I liked Mrs. Young. An attractive brunette in her late thirties, widow of a wealthy financier, she was well read, widely travelled, and knew a lot of important people. However, something about her put Jeanne off, and so we saw little more of the woman or her friends. That was a great disappointment to me. I'm not sure what the problem was, but it could have been the way she had introduced Jeanne to one of those friends: "This is my war effort!" Jeanne later commented to me, "I guess I must have been a great effort for her!" However, if that was a poor choice of words on the part of the hostess, it rivals a comment an otherwise intelligent and polite CWAC made when Mrs. Young offered her a drink: "No, thanks, we're not professional drinkers in Canada!" How gauche some of us kids were.

Sometime that fall Jeanne and I found another intriguing venue, the International Club. Many of the members were civilians, some from backgrounds unexpected. Thus it was that one evening I found myself dancing with a civilian with a guttural accent.

"Where are you from?" I asked.

"Heidelberg." He smiled at the surprised expression on my face. I thought at first he was joking, but his accent and the details he then provided gave his story some credibility. He told me he'd spent a year at an internment camp in Canada. Were there sometimes situations where a POW was determined later to be a refugee? I wondered, but before I could question him further, the dance ended and he made a beeline for a stunning-looking blonde who had just entered the room.

Events listing for the International Youth Centre.

It must have been a member of the International Club who was responsible for a mysterious letter I found among my papers several years ago. At the top was a London W.1 address, suggesting a fashionable area. The letter reads as follows:

Dear Miss:
I would be pleased to help you with your French.
I am French ex Army Officer and have a lovely
apartment and am free most evenings.
Please reply so we can meet and be friend.
Yours,
Marcel

Since I have absolutely no memory of receiving that letter, I assume I did not favour Marcel with a reply. I must have placed a notice on the club bulletin board, indicating my interest in finding someone to converse with in French, and this was the result. What a shame I didn't answer; I might now be living in Paris and speaking perfect French! On the other hand, Marcel might have turned out to be a real rogue. The mention of the "lovely apartment" could well have alerted me to that possibility.

I am reminded here of the case of "The Amorous Pole." He stands out because he was the only Polish fellow I was to meet during my sojourn in England, although I have since read that there were many Polish Air Force pilots in the U.K. flying alongside the RAF. Lil had met this fellow on a bus one day, and subsequently been asked to bring a friend along and come to dinner at his hotel. And so it happened that on a rare Saturday when neither of us had anything better to do, we arrived for dinner at the Russell Hotel.[2]

Our Polish pilot met us in the lobby and invited us up to his room for drinks. We looked at each other, both thinking the same thing: there are two of us and only one of him, so what harm can come of it? That was pretty naïve on our part. He could have had one or more of his pals lying in wait. Luckily, he didn't. He turned out to be hard enough to handle all by himself. He had in mind a tryst à trois. We fought him off, treated it all as a huge joke, and complained about being hungry until he acted like a proper host and took us down to dinner. We ate well, thanked him graciously, and went home, declining the invitation to his room for after-dinner drinks.

Soon after that, Lil and I had a much more satisfactory encounter. Sitting in a pub, we were suddenly bedazzled by the enormous amount of gold braid decorating the uniforms of three gentlemen who came to sit with us: an Aussie merchant navy captain and his two senior officers. They took us out several evenings in a row before their leave ended and they were again off to sea. Thus began a very pleasant year-long association. Every two or three months, I would get a phone call and we would again spend a few evenings in their company, dining, chatting, sometimes taking in a movie or a play. They were quiet, serious fellows, not at all flirtatious, just in need of a break from the rigours of their dangerous life at sea. We would always meet them in the lobby of the Regent's Palace, a popular hotel in the heart of the theatre district. I wonder what happened to those men. Merchant Navy men got a raw deal after the war. At least they did in Canada. They had suffered high casualties, running most of the risks of the regular Navy, going back and forth across the seas, ferrying much-needed supplies, but were denied the post-war benefits of the military services. It took years for them to receive any compensation.

CHAPTER EIGHT

SETTLING INTO THE WARTIME ROUTINE

MY ROOMMATES at 13 Stanhope Terrace were quite a mix. Despite the mix, or perhaps because of it, we lived together fairly comfortably, with only the occasional disagreement. Three were several years older than the rest of us: Holly, twenty-seven, married and the epitome of gentility without being "stuffy," contrasted sharply with Mary, well into her thirties, whose blunt language and suspected relationships with the opposite sex set her somewhat apart. Holly became close friends with Anne, a tall slender blonde, twenty-five, the only driver in our group. Dot, small, awkward, and rather prim, seeming young for her alleged age of twenty-one, viewed the buxom, brazen Mary with an especially jaundiced eye. Jeanne, who was to become my lifelong friend, held very strong and at times unusual and unexpected views on many things and didn't hesitate to voice them. Only much later did I discover that although she had been a CWAC a full year and a half prior to being posted overseas, Jeanne certainly was the youngest of us all and would not have her twenty-first birthday until November 1943. Some thought her judgmental, but her originality intrigued me.

Jeanne was the only one I recall playing the occasional practical joke on us. Most were harmless, but I do remember one that gave everyone a jolt. I was tiptoeing into the room after Lights Out, trying hard to be quiet and not wake anybody, feeling my way along, when suddenly a cold wet cloth slammed into my face. My ear-piercing shriek and Jeanne's ensuing raucous laugh woke the entire house. None of us were too happy at the time, but we laughed about it later. I remember another occasion when a blood-curdling scream woke everyone up, this one not the result of a prank. Someone quickly turned on the light. Dot was yelling, "I can't find my bed!" Her whole body had taken a ninety-degree turn. There she was, lying across her narrow cot, legs kicking out madly on one side, head and arms on the other, frantically pawing the air like someone on a flutter board, thrashing about in air rather than water. We all expressed sympathy and set about comforting her, suppressing the impulse to laugh.

We seldom if ever discussed our jobs, not because they involved any need for secrecy, but because most were just plain boring. Except for Dot, whose clerical ineptitude had led to demotion to "general duties," which included such things as scrubbing floors and washing dishes, and Anne, the driver, we were all junior clerks.

Anne was the only person who did at times regale us with tales of her work. She had the sole truly interesting job. How I envied her! Driving around wartime London could not have been easy, and occasionally she would be called out at night and have to cope with the blackout and possible air raids. She also had to spend one day a week in greasy coveralls, doing vehicle maintenance. But I didn't consider all that. I thought only about all the places she was seeing, the people she was transporting, the fact that she never knew from day to day what would happen next, the stories she had to tell.

One time, Anne and a fellow CWAC had picked up some medical supplies from a London depot for delivery to a military camp some twenty or thirty miles south of the city. Their cargo included 5,000 "safes." That's what they called condoms in those days.[1] At destination, the receiving medical corporal counted only 4,000. "How the hell did you two girls go through a thousand of these things in an hour?" he teased. Ironically, Anne later became pregnant, a terrible disgrace for a girl in those days, and one that risked getting a servicewoman a dishonourable discharge. Fortunately her boyfriend from home, who happened not to be the baby's father, came knowingly to the rescue and married her, well before the pregnancy became obvious. I hope that marriage worked out.[2]

Looking back, we all got along surprisingly well. Holly, the most mature, knew how to defuse confrontations with wise counsel and calm approach. Anne used gentle humour to equal advantage. I remember one time when Jeanne and Mary exchanged verbal insults. I don't know what Jeanne had done to annoy her, but Mary shouted, "What's the matter with you, Jeanne? You need someone to teach you the facts of life!" Jeanne shot back, "No doubt you've been taught them many times!" Ouch.

Confrontations were most apt to develop between Mary and Dot, both of whom had short fuses. One morning in particular, use of our one bathroom became a huge issue. Several of the girls resented Dot's "hogging" of the bathroom. She was the only one who went in there to dress, and what was worse, she always locked the door. The rest of us would lock the door on occasion, but for as brief a time as possible. Since we girls had a mere forty-five minutes after reveille to use the toilet, wash, dress, fix hair and face, and dash across the square to the dining hall for breakfast at 0715 hours, the bathroom was much in demand. On this occasion, when Dot had spent more time than usual in the locked "loo," Mary exploded, hammering on the door with both fists and shouting, "What in hell's the matter with you, Dot? Are you a man, trying to pass as one of us?"

I sometimes wondered whether it would have been better to have no lock at all on the bathroom door. However, in another London barracks where that was the case, the lack of a lock brought its own set of problems. The girls were forever walking in on each other, sometimes in error, sometimes as a joke. One girl, fed up with this intrusion on her privacy, decided to keep a basin full of water beside the tub. One Saturday morning, just as she was settling down to a relaxing bath, there was a knock on the door, preceded by the call "Duty Officer!" The girl grabbed the basin and hurled it full force at the door as it opened. This time it was no joke. The dripping-wet officer was not happy. The girl was paraded to the commanding officer the next day, but fortunately that worthy person had a sense of humour and good-naturedly dismissed her with the warning "Don't do that again!"

The English had various names for what we Canadians commonly call the "bathroom" or the "washroom." They might say the "loo" or the "WC" (water closet) or, less commonly, the "lavatory." Someone might say, "I have to spend a penny," a reference to fees commonly charged in public lavatories. Americans often used a different term. Once, in a British Army canteen, a WAC (member of the American Women's Army Corps) bewildered the civilian volunteer behind the counter by asking directions to the "restroom." Luckily I was standing nearby to interpret.

That was neither the first nor last time I would find myself explaining the Americans to the British and vice versa. It wasn't only the minor matter of differences in terminology. Attitudes were often different, and clashes were bound to occur from time to time. Americans sometimes mistook British polite restraint for snobbishness, and the British tended to see American flag-waving and bluntness as arrogance and boorishness. The fact that American service personnel received substantially higher pay than their British counterparts did not help the relationship any.

Canadian military personnel were better off than the British, but still played second fiddle to the Americans in terms of pay and amenities. American soldiers were described as "over-paid, over-sexed, and over here!" That reminds me of another saying, attributed to Canadian and American soldiers who acquired English girlfriends. When the girl back home would ask, "What has she got that I haven't got?" the soldier would write back, "Nothing. But she's got it here!"

We usually attended dances at the service clubs or, if outside London, at various Canadian Army camps, but one night Jeanne and I decided to go to a dance at a nearby British Army barracks. Arriving late, we took our places in the middle of a long row of empty chairs. The antics of the dancers amazed us. Never before had we witnessed such manoeuvres. Both partners faced in the same direction for a few steps, then the man would twirl the woman around so that they would be facing in opposite directions for a few more steps, and so on, back and forth. Having had great difficulty learning to dance at all, I was sure I wouldn't be able to perform this complicated procedure.

Luckily, when the music started again, Jeanne was the one asked to dance. At the first twirl she tripped over the fellow's foot and would have fallen headlong had he not grabbed her. I, the lone wallflower and for once glad of that status, fought valiantly to suppress a fit of giggles. It was hopeless. All I could do was pretend a coughing fit. I fooled no one, least of all Jeanne, as she continued to stumble around the floor, cheeks burning with embarrassment. Escorted back to her chair, she hissed at me, "Just wait until someone asks you to dance!"

I was hoping no one would, but almost immediately an unsuspecting young man approached and led me onto the floor. With the advantage of longer observation time, I did slightly better than Jeanne, but not much. When the music stopped, we both fled the hall. We had disgraced Canadian womanhood enough. We walked back to barracks chuckling to ourselves despite the sudden wail of the air-raid siren.

My most frightening experience in London had nothing to do with air raids. During World War II, the majority of English homes and buildings were still heated by coal fires. On occasion, the soot thus generated combined with the heavily moisturized air to create a fog so dense that one could see little beyond arm's length: the traditional London "pea-souper." Although I knew my short route from the bus stop well, on this particular foggy evening, hurrying home for supper, I must have taken a wrong turn. Suddenly I had no idea where I was. Lost, cold, tired, and hungry, I panicked. In desperation I felt my way along building walls, every so often having to navigate around a staircase and then find a continuation of the wall. And then there came a point where my arms were reaching out in vain, hands pawing the air. Was I at a street corner? But if so, what corner? I could neither hear nor see a thing.

The fog muffled sounds of traffic. I was shaking with fear, heart pounding. All of a sudden I bumped into a solid but resilient object with a Cockney accent. Thank heaven for that air-raid warden! "Just you hang on to me, love, and I'll take you right to your door," he assured me, as he tucked my arm in his. Having heard my accent, and being thoroughly familiar with the area, he was as good as his word. As it turned out, 13 Stanhope Terrace was only a block away. Never was I so relieved to get into the light and warmth of barracks.

CHAPTER NINE

HIGHS AND LOWS

BY THE SUMMER of 1943, a number of us had acquired bicycles. Many, like mine, were army discards and therefore men's bikes. Ken had given me mine when I visited his camp in Surrey one spring weekend. That rusty and very basic machine became my most treasured possession, carrying me on many a jaunt to various parts of the United Kingdom over the next couple of years.

I was eager to explore the country, visiting sites familiar from history and literature and tales told by my English parents. It was a unique opportunity. Never again would one be able to wander at any time of day through quiet and almost empty streets in towns like Oxford and Cambridge and Stratford-upon-Avon, or in any season enter as sole visitor the homes of such literary greats as Robbie Burns or

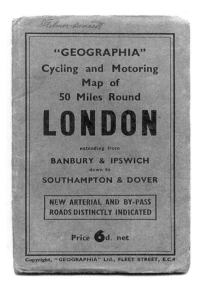

Our map used
on cycling trips.

Shakespeare or Thomas Hardy. Free from today's traffic and throngs of sightseers, one could linger in the quiet, soaking up the atmosphere, imagining one's self back in centuries past.

A few snapshots from memory: in Canterbury the ancient gate arching over the roadway, the five-hundred-year-old inn nearby, the majestic cathedral, all seen through a veil of steady rain that dampened our spirits not in the least; Salisbury Cathedral with its distinctive embroidered-stone spire and awe-inspiring cloisters; on the south coast, near Lewes Castle, the peaceful Downs on a warm, sunny afternoon so heavenly that the war seemed unreal; by contrast, Princes Street in Edinburgh, with the Walter Scott Monument, the castle on guard above, on a damp and chilly September afternoon.

In August of 1943, I gave my recently acquired bicycle its first long test run. Stephanie and I set off on a history/literature tour, over the Cotswold Hills with their amber-coloured stone villages, through Oxford with its "dreaming spires," and on to Stratford-upon-Avon, through Warwick and its castles, circling back through Cambridge and Banbury Cross and so to London. My agenda for the trip was simply to visit as many of the historic places as possible, given our tight budget, nine-day time limit, and self-powered transportation. Stephanie, who had also enlisted in Vancouver and come over with me on the *Queen Elizabeth*, had a different goal. She suffered through my agenda only because she wanted company on the trip, whose objective for her was connecting with an American boyfriend stationed near Warwick. I browsed around the town during her brief time with him. It could not have been a happy time, for she was back within a couple of hours, looking quite downcast. She never spoke of him again, and I thought it best to ask no questions.

Selfishly, I put my companion's problems out of my mind and continued to enjoy what was for me a great experience. After Stratford-upon-Avon and Oxford, we explored the intact and impressive Warwick Castle; the contrasting nearby ruins of Kenilworth Castle, whose duke chose the wrong side in the English Civil War (and paid for his error by having his castle wrecked while neighbouring Warwick Castle escaped unscathed); and Cambridge with its grassy "backs" and river. I was particularly interested in Cambridge, because my paternal grandfather had obtained two degrees there, in law and then theology, before going on to enjoy a long and happy calling as an Anglican minister.

East Hornden,
13 August 43.

Dear Mother:

Just a few lines to you before I drop off to sleep. I'm sitting up in a nice comfortable bed, having spent the last hour or so in the bath tub trying to soak some of the dirt collected on the trip off of me. It wasn't always easy to find a place to stay, let alone a place to have a good hot bath. However, here at Stue's aunt's home, we're enjoying solid comfort.

We're on the last lap of our journey now, as this little place is only about 18 miles from London — thought we'd get back there by tomorrow night, and so leave ourselves a day to rest up. I never thought this would take so much out of us, but then I hadn't counted on so many hills and such a strong wind against us the whole time. Right now it's only five after nine and I'm dead tired even tho' we cycled only about 40 miles today.

Had planned to see St. Albans on our way back but it's a bit far from here and we're pretty tired. Did travel through the Cotswold Country between Oxford and Stratford-on-Avon — certainly is pretty — lovely little villages. Unfortunately it was too dull to take any snaps but maybe I'll get up there some week-end, after I recover financially. Stone broke right now! We've been away a week tomorrow and living isn't exactly cheap these days. Having to buy a new bike, & getting my raincoat stolen — oh well, it's been worth it!

A letter to my mother from the end of our cycling trip,
lamenting the theft of my raincoat.

We also made a couple of side trips. Seeing the appealing name "Saffron Walden" on the map, I insisted we go there. With a name like that it had to be a gem! And it was, nestled in a pretty little valley. We stayed overnight in its hostel, a building we were told dated back four centuries. It was my idea also to go a few miles out of our way to see Rupert Brooke's beloved Grantchester. In my last year of high school, I had written a lengthy essay about Brooke and memorized every one of his poems. As we approached the little village I recited a couple of my favourite lines to Stephanie:

Ah God! to see the branches stir
Across the moon at Grantchester!

In retrospect, I suspect my companion, who had never heard of Rupert Brooke, couldn't have been less interested. We didn't see the sun, let alone the moon, at Grantchester, but I was happy to find the small, surprisingly plain village church (unfortunately not open) and noted Brooke's name, listed with some dozen or two others, on the equally plain war memorial in front of it. Sadly, he had been accorded no special recognition as a literary great. He was just another villager who had given his life for King and country in the First World War.

c◊o

In October I received a note from Ken to say he'd been injured in a training exercise and was in a military hospital in Surrey. I took Jeanne with me to visit him. We arrived by train in the tiny village, hungry for lunch. There were only two tea shops, both in the same block on the one and only street. Jeanne poked her nose in the first. "What do you have to eat?" she asked.

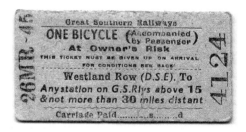

A train ticket for my bicycle.

"Spam and chips," the proprietor called out from the back of the shop.

"Oh, hell!" said Jeanne.

The man exploded: "What's the matter with you girls? Don't you know there's a war on?"

Well, I should think we did know! Here we were, thousands of miles from home, in uniform, CANADA insignia on our shoulders. What a silly thing for him to say! We went along to the second shop, where we ate…Spam and chips! When you're young and hungry, you will eat anything.

Ken was in a ward with several other Canadian Army officers, each recovering from some apparently fairly minor injury. They all seemed glad to see us, but they'd have been glad to see almost anyone. In this out-of-the-way village they would not have had many visitors. At one point the nurse asked us to leave the room while she administered the daily injections. That was the first time I had heard of penicillin. It was then very new and administered by a shot in the rear end. In this particular case, the nurse told us, it was being used to prevent possible infection rather than treat it. I was happy to see Ken in good spirits and recovering well.

Another weekend I went on my own to see Ken, still in hospital. I enjoyed a couple of visits with him, but on that occasion I especially appreciated the hospitality of a retired British Army major and his wife who, like so many of their compatriots, were in the habit of generously entertaining service personnel in their homes. On Saturday evening, after dinner, this kindly couple took me over to visit Sir Harry Britton, retired British MP and, so he told me, good friend of R.B. Bennett, former prime minister of Canada. We spent a pleasant evening comparing life and customs in our respective countries.

A letter to my brother a fortnight later tells of an experience earlier that same week. From time to time, the Army would relieve the tedium of our dull jobs by sending a select few on a current affairs course. I don't know on what basis the selection was made, but in this particular case, we three or four CWACs were the only attendees below officer rank. Most of the speakers were scholars of high calibre, but we also heard from high-ranking British military officers, the BBC's chief foreign service broadcaster, and a Frenchman who enthralled us with terrifying details of his escape from France in the spring of that year. I can't remember whether or not courses like this were optional, but starved as I was for a little intellectual stimulation, I seized every opportunity that came my way.

In the same letter, I apologize to my brother for the delay in writing. Shortly after that weekend visit to Ken, I'd had a tooth extracted. It was only a wisdom tooth, but this being my first extraction ever, I assumed the severe pain that evening to be a normal consequence. "Here, Doris, take one of these," Dot offered, pill in hand. Her pharmacist father had sent her overseas with an arsenal of medications. I had no idea what this pill was, but desperately gulped it down. The next morning, still in pain, I gratefully accepted two more of Dot's pills, and another two or three that evening. Not until the third day, by then in a complete daze after still another pill, did I stumble back to the army dentist, who promptly diagnosed a dry socket and plugged up the hole with something or other, instantly banishing the pain. I later discovered Dot had been happily dispensing tablets containing codeine!

Alas, that was not to be the last of my health problems. I could not have been very good company during much of that second winter in London. The monotony of the job had plunged me into a kind of depression. For a time I withdrew into myself, avoided socializing with my civilian co-workers at the Records Office during the day, and stayed holed up in our room after work, at least during the week.

Although I kept a mostly cheery note in my letters home, my medical records reveal one malady after another, all winter long. I was at a low ebb physically as well as mentally. One dreary November day, I noticed a slightly itchy rash on the left side of my forehead. My left eye felt sore as well. It happened to be one of my on-duty Saturdays at the Records Office, and so I dropped by Captain Brown's office. "Ever had measles?" he asked. "No, sir." He took my temperature. "Well, it's not that. I think you've got shingles." Whereupon he gave me an eye shield to wear and ordered me to the infirmary, within our barracks, for an extended stay—"at least a couple of weeks."

Since I felt only slightly off-key and suffered almost no pain,

I didn't realize how serious this ailment could be or its significance. I certainly didn't appreciate the risk to my vision and only later discovered how rare shingles was for someone my age. My immunity must have been low. Silly girl that I was, I worried primarily about my date for that evening. I felt sorry for the nice Canadian corporal who was taking the train some thirty or so miles to come into town and take me out. Since I had no way to contact him, there was nothing for it but to await his arrival and lean out of the infirmary's second-storey window to express my apologies. Two or three minutes, and then the corporal on duty in the infirmary ordered me away from the window.

My sixteen days of forced confinement bored me almost to tears. Other girls came and went, mostly with bad colds and staying only two or three days. Other than chatting with them, I had nothing to do, except sometimes listen to the radio. I tried to read now and again, but my one available eye soon tired. And so it happened that when a Canadian woman war correspondent arrived to interview us, I griped at great length: "I'm just bored to death here. My job is horrible, too, dull as dishwater, but at least when I'm working I can get out in the evenings." A few weeks later, my mother sent me a clipping from the *Vancouver Sun*. I read it in shock, resolving never again to believe anything in the newspapers, at least "for the duration." I suppose the poor woman could hardly send in what I actually said, but she could have avoided misquoting me so blatantly, instead of having me say, "It's so lovely and comfortable here I just don't want to leave!" She didn't have to tell such a whopping big lie. She could have instead commented on the colourful cover Jeanne had made for my eye patch, bright pink with a skull-and-cross-bones design.

I returned to work rested but hardly refreshed. One day I was puzzled to find the sergeant-major working beside me all day, doing the same kind of copying job I was doing. At the end of it, he confessed that he'd been asked to spy on me by one of the officers, who thought I was falling down on the job. The sergeant-major, a kindly older man, said he admired my "beautiful penmanship," could see I'd worked hard the whole day, and would report accordingly. Of course, with him beside me I hadn't taken the usual time out to read extraneous interesting material in the files. The incident gave me a bit of a jolt, since Dot had been doing the same sort of work before her demotion to general duties, which meant scrubbing barracks floors and other menial tasks. She said the work wasn't so bad, since you could think of all sorts of other things when scrubbing floors, but she regretted the loss of status and especially trades pay, and was never going to let her parents at home know what had happened. I decided I had better make a greater effort to avoid the same fate and resigned myself to trying to concentrate on this boring job.

Canadian Press Staff Writer

LONDON, Dec. 16 (Advance)— In a Canadian Women's Army Corps barracks near Hyde Park, the sick bay was a gay, warm place, and the patients were cheerful, in spite of a mild 'flu epidemic.

Sgt. Helen Hunley of Calgary and Cpl. Helen Barndart of Vancouver were reading in bed.

Pte. Doris Filmer-Bennet of Vancouver was able to be up and sit in front of the fire in her housecoat. "It is so comfortable I don't want to leave," she said, stretching her legs lazily.

The medical corporal, Dorothy Hook of Regina, explained that sick bay is just for mild cases. For anything more serious than a cold the girls go to a Canadian military hospital.

The officers' quarters are in a similar house on the same street. Two officers share a large room and there are modern bathrooms done in tile.

The drawing room downstairs was as attractive and smart as one in a posh London home.

The officers were gathering around the piano. Lt. Faith Cornwall of Victoria, Lt. Phyllis Agger of Winnipeg and others were practicing Christmas carols. They will sing them in a children's hospital.

A *Vancouver Sun* article totally misrepresenting my situation in London.

I looked forward to my next leave, this time one of the "educational leaves" available to servicemen and women. These were set up under various auspices and provided a wonderful respite from deadly dull military routines. A couple of weeks before Christmas I took a train to Southampton for a week-long stay at the University of Southampton's School of Navigation, made available during the naval cadets' Christmas break.

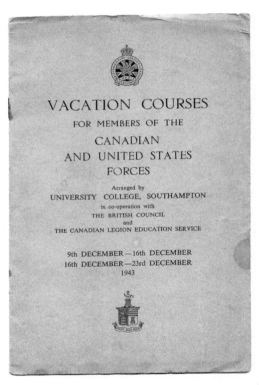

A listing of the vacation courses
available to the Armed Forces at the
University of Southampton.

A friendship begun during that leave endured longer than most. The second day I was there, along with several WACs (our American counterparts) and a dozen or more Canadian and American soldiers, in marched a couple of platoons of Canadian Army officer cadets, Trev among them. He was pleasant looking and fairly tall, with kindly, twinkling blue eyes. What impressed me most was his honest, open manner, thoughtfulness, and intelligent conversation. He seemed really interested in my opinions. By comparison, many of the men I had met overseas up to that point talked endlessly of themselves and expected you to hang on their every word.

The cadets stayed only three days, but long enough for Trev and me to become good friends. During our free time in the evenings we chatted non-stop. On his last night we went into town to see the Bette Davis film *Now, Voyager*, a movie I will always associate with Trev. Like the film's hero, Trev was married and told me so on first meeting. While our situation differed in many respects from that of the movie protagonists, over time we became sufficiently fond of each other for the relationship to develop some overtones of their bittersweet romance. At the end of Trev's three days, I had to wave him farewell and settle down to enjoying the remainder of this busy sightseeing week in and around Portsmouth and Southampton.

Each day we were taken on the navigation school's bus to a number of historic spots and entertained by some remarkable people. Among these were Lady Mountbatten and her older daughter, Patricia, who had graciously invited us to Broadlands, their estate in Romsey in the New Forest. We Canadians, who should have learned about the New Forest from our exposure to British history in school, were just as surprised as the Americans to discover that it was not a forest at all. Instead, it was and is a vast expanse of land encompassing both woodland and farmland, with a number of small hamlets and villages.

Broadlands, a large estate with a Palladian-style stately home, had been in Lady Mountbatten's family since late Victorian times. At the time of our visit, Broadlands—like so many other such estates—was suffering the effects of the war. Lady Edwina Mountbatten and her daughter, both slim, attractive brunettes, greeted us on the steps. Both looked the part of English landed gentry, dressed in typical country style: tweed jackets and skirts and sturdy oxfords.

Lady Mountbatten asked if we would care to tour the property before tea and then led us through rough fields of ankle-deep grass down a gentle slope towards the river and over to areas where idle fountains remained as lonely relics of once flourishing gardens. I was reminded of Swinburne's "The Forsaken Garden" except that these were far inland and so did not sweep to "the sea-down's edge." In wartime no one was available to keep up such extensive gardens and grounds. Thus the situation would remain for the duration of the war and longer. How often during our stay in England we were to hear that phrase, "for the duration." The blackout would continue, rationing would continue, shortages would continue, we Canadians would remain overseas "for the duration." It began to seem like forever.

As on most days at that time of year, the weather was cool and cloudy, with the ever-present threat of showers. Luckily the rain held off until we were safely ensconced in what in

That's me in the front row, far left, Pat on the far right. Our arm bands spell CWAC.

Ken, UBC Library, spring 1941. Briefly a boyfriend, he enlisted and went overseas before I did and was a trusted friend and confidant for most of my time there.

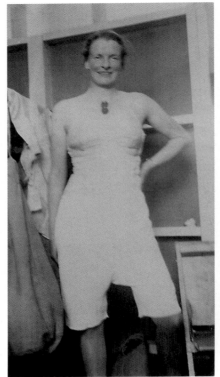

ABOVE LEFT: Proud of new uniform, ashamed of newly cropped hair, with friend Fran in downtown Vancouver. Street photo, August 1942.

ABOVE RIGHT: Sally modelling army underwear, a dubious luxury issued to CWACs on overseas draft. Argyle Barracks, Ottawa, early December 1942.

RIGHT: Donning a life jacket in the *Queen Elizabeth* cabin, December 1942.

With my gutsy friend Phyllis, somewhere in Devon, May 1943.

With Lil and her U.S. Marine (my Marine date is taking the photo).
Hyde Park, March 1943.

With Stephanie, who came overseas with me on the *Queen Elizabeth*, at Kenilworth Castle, Warwickshire, August 1943.

My glamorous roommate, Sunny. Late summer, 1944.

RIGHT: On the steps of 13 Stanhope Terrace, Lancaster Gate, with my English roommate Pat, spring 1944. Photo by Jeanne White.

Trev in front of the statue *Physical Energy*, Kensington Gardens, January 1944.

Jeanne, self-portrait, Christmas 1943, in the room we shared with four or five other CWACs at 13 Stanhope Terrace.

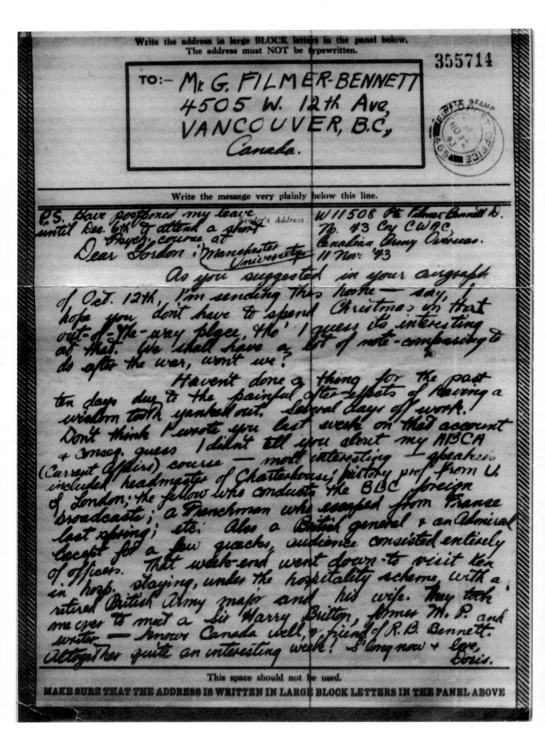

Write the address in large BLOCK letters in the panel below.
The address must NOT be typewritten.

355714

TO:- Mr G. FILMER-BENNETT
4505 W. 12th Ave,
VANCOUVER, B.C.,
Canada.

Write the message very plainly below this line.

P.S. Have postponed my leave
until Dec. 6th & attend a short
Psych. course at
Manchester University.

Sender's Address: W 11508 Pte Filmer-Bennett D.
No. 43 Coy C.W.A.C.,
Canadian Army Overseas.
11 Nov: '43

Dear Gordon:

As you suggested in your airgraph
of Oct. 12th, I'm sending this home — say, I
hope you don't have to spend Christmas in that
out-of-the-way place, tho' I guess its interesting
at that. We shall have a lot of note-comparing to
do after the war, won't we?

Haven't done a thing for the past
ten days due to the painful after-effects of having a
wisdom tooth yanked out. Several days off work.
Don't think I wrote you last week on that account
& smog. guess I didn't tell you about my ABCA
(Current Affairs) course — most interesting — speakers
included headmaster of Charterhouse; history prof from U.
of London; the fellow who conducts the BBC foreign
broadcasts; a Frenchman who escaped from France
last spring; etc. Also a British general & an Admiral
(except for a few quacks, audience consisted entirely
of officers. That week-end went down to visit Ken
in hosp. staying, under the hospitality scheme, with a
retired British Army major and his wife. They took
me over to meet a Sir Harry Britton, former M.P. and
writer — knows Canada well, friend of R.B. Bennett.
Altogether quite an interesting week! So long now & love,
Doris.

This space should not be used.
MAKE SURE THAT THE ADDRESS IS WRITTEN IN LARGE BLOCK LETTERS IN THE PANEL ABOVE

Airgraph letter to my brother. Written on regular-size paper, these letters
were then much reduced in size by the postal service. Being long-winded,
I wrote most of my letters home on the thin blue airmail forms instead.

Canadian Armoured Corps sergeant major, Women's Army Corps (U.S.) private, U.S. Army sergeant, and myself on a School of Navigation tour, with the spire of Salisbury Cathedral in the background, December 1943.

Hyde Park, April 1944. Photo by Jeanne White.

With Trev in front of the Albert Memorial, near Royal Albert Hall, London, January 1944.

With Cay (in front) and Gen in the driveway beside our Selection of Personnel Office hut, HQ CRU, April 1945.

Studio portrait, Stratford-upon-Avon, June 1944. Strangely serious!

ABOVE LEFT: Millie, sergeant major of 47 Company, in Grant Square, Farnborough, September 1944, her shared living quarters in the background.

ABOVE RIGHT: Taking it easy with New Zealand friends while Cookie does most of the work, Stratford-upon-Avon, June 1944.

RIGHT: Punting on the Basingstoke Canal at a Selection of Personnel Office picnic, May 1945. I am at the helm.

ABOVE LEFT: Gen, myself, and Aileen at our Selection of Personnel Office window, Farnborough, late 1944.

ABOVE RIGHT: Reggie, studio portrait, July 1945.

LEFT: Charles Joyce from Manitoba, one of the fine young men who paused briefly at CRU en route to battle in early 1945.

ABOVE LEFT: With Major Brewer and Gen on a London weekend, in front of the Peter Pan statue, Kensington Gardens, early June 1945.

ABOVE RIGHT: With my trusty bicycle, wearing George's beret, somewhere in Éire, March 1945. Photo by Jeanne White.

RIGHT: With Jeanne in Dublin, street photo, March 1945.

Jeanne, January 1945. Self-portrait.

Buying cockles and winkles at Brighton, the weekend after VE Day. (George had just given me the battledress jacket.) Photo by Jeanne White.

Lost in the Mountains of Mourne, bordering Éire, supposedly en route to Belfast. Photo by Jeanne White.

ABOVE LEFT: Hitchhiking from Ramsgate to Dover, still wearing George's jacket, June 1945, wielding workman/driver's shovel for dramatic effect. Photo by Jeanne White.

ABOVE RIGHT: 13 Stanhope Terrace, taken by the author in the 1980s.

RIGHT: Outside a restaurant in Dunlear, Éire, not far from the Ulster border. Photo by Jeanne White.

The HQ CRU sergeants: Millie front row far right, myself back row second CWAC from left, Gen fourth; Andy Beck third from left in second row, Bill (mess administrator) third from right in front row. (Reggie is absent, probably away on leave.)

Dover Beach, June 1945. I gaze longingly across the Channel
to the French coast: "If only we had been able to get over there!"
My favourite portrait, by Jeanne White.

ordinary times might have been the morning room, where Lady Mountbatten and her daughter themselves served a delicious afternoon tea. It wasn't the lavish spread of pre-war days, when as well as dainty cucumber and watercress sandwiches, guests would have been treated to scones heaped with Devonshire cream and preserves, sugary meringues, and more, but the open-faced pâté sandwiches and warm baking powder biscuits were tasty and nutritious and satisfying. Indeed, later studies showed the British to have been healthier on wartime diets than in pre-war days, when no shortages had existed, at least for those with adequate funds.

We saw no evidence of servants, although a cook must have been tucked away in the kitchen. The biggest change, however, was in the house itself. Lady Mountbatten turned and waved at the wall behind her chair. "There is a military hospital on the other side of that wall," she said. "We had the wall put in two years ago. It extends from the front to the rear of the house, cutting it almost exactly in half." This was not the only stately home to serve military purposes during the Second World War.

It was fitting that guests of the navigation school, like us, should be entertained at the Mountbatten estate, since Lord Mountbatten at this point held the rank of rear admiral in the British Navy. We felt greatly honoured. We were also a little awestruck, but our hostesses welcomed us warmly and engaged us in conversation so effortlessly as to quickly put us all at ease. An American officer with our group later conceded: "When it comes to social know-how, you've gotta hand it to the British aristocracy. These guys have sure got style."

Another day we were entertained on board a British battleship. Remembering the way we, as CWAC other ranks, had been segregated from the officers on the *Queen Elizabeth* coming over, I was pleased to find that the British Navy had no such qualms about fraternization. So far as they were concerned, we were "ladies" and, as such, entitled to be entertained in the wardroom by the ship's officers. (Later I wondered whether we were accepted out of courtesy because we were not English. Would British Wrens below officer status have been treated as liberally?)

I remember a lively cocktail party, with animated conversation, a wealth of tasty sandwiches and canapés, and free-flowing liquor. I followed my usual routine of making one glass last indefinitely, resisting offers to top it up. That way I could focus my attention on the goings-on around me and avoid adverse after-effects as well as any risk of disgracing the Corps.

Regrettably, I focused almost completely on the handsome young officers rather than on the battleship. For security reasons I did not mention it in my letters home, so today I cannot recall its name.

CHAPTER TEN

THE BUILD-UP TO D-DAY

I DON'T REMEMBER much about Christmas 1943. I do recall spending it in barracks, where we were served an excellent Christmas dinner with all the trimmings in the festively decorated mess hall. We each received a little package of goodies from the Red Cross. Jeanne had just returned from her leave at that time, staying with a kindly British family somewhere in the country. A number of others spent the holiday with English relatives. Many of our girls were of British parentage, with aunts and uncles, cousins, and sometimes grandparents in the U.K.

The pleasant Canadian officer cadet I had met at the University of Southampton's School of Navigation lost no time in coming to see me. Trev came up to London a couple of times in January, once on his own, the second time with a

fellow cadet, an equally pleasant chap. Since Ken also made
the trip another weekend, January was a busy month. It would
have been a wonderful month but for a persistent cold I could
not seem to shake. Trev came again in February, on a couple
of weekends. I enjoyed his company very much, particularly
since, like me, he loved the theatre and we usually took in a
play or two. I also remember enjoying a concert by the U.S.
Army Negro Chorus. I always felt very relaxed with Trev. The

Trev and I enjoyed hearing the
U.S. Army Negro Chorus.

fact that he was married meant that there could be no emotional entanglement to complicate things. Or so I thought.

With Ken, the relationship was different. While we were just friends, rather than boyfriend and girlfriend as we had been during the one year at UBC, the past relationship was always there in the background. Ken still thought of me as the timid soul I had been, not the more autonomous young woman I was in the process of becoming. He was the one calling the shots, making the decisions as to what we would be doing. Trev, on the other hand, held me in high esteem, was sensitive to my feelings, and always asked me what I would like to do. He was also of a gentler nature than Ken. I in turn had a great deal of respect for Trev. Having become aware of the sleaziness of many American and Canadian married soldiers, some of whom went so far as to show their dates phony pay books identifying them as single, I appreciated the fact that he had told me about his wife back home the first time we met.

One day in late February, after a particularly heavy air raid during the night, I arrived at work to see two immense craters across the street. Little trace remained of the two houses that had been there the day before. Our large, sprawling building appeared intact, but many of the windows had been blown out and we had no heat. We CWACs in our heavy greatcoats stayed warmer than many of the civilians, but soon our hands were blue with cold and we had to keep rubbing them together. It was a great relief when early in the afternoon our superiors themselves could no longer stand the cold and closed up shop for the day.

The next morning I awoke with a stuffy nose and sore

throat. By the time I left for work, the cold had invaded my chest. Every cough hurt like the devil. I dragged myself to the still frigid Records Office, where a shivering, sneezing Captain Brown promptly diagnosed bronchitis and ordered me to the No. 10 Canadian General Hospital near Watford. Well, at least I would have another respite from the job!

The hospital stay did little to cure my bronchitis. Oh, it did some good, and then it quickly undid the good it had done. After a few days of forced bedrest I felt almost completely well. However, as an ambulatory patient I then had to help care for the bedridden patients, carrying food trays to and from the kitchen. Had the building been a modern edifice, well insulated and evenly heated, that might have presented no problem. However, this century-old former "insane asylum" had overheated wards and long, cold, drafty corridors through which you could almost hear the winter wind whistling. It was just my luck to be in the ward farthest from the kitchen. I returned to work sicker than when I'd left. Captain Brown banged his fist on the desk in disgust. "That's the last time I send anyone to that hospital," he vowed.[1] "Give this to your commanding officer," he said, signing an order asking that I be sent on leave at the earliest possible date. "You need to get out into the country for a while."

Captain Brown was absolutely right. The leave beginning a few days later in the sunny Cornwall countryside marked a turning point in my health and mood. What good fortune that my host turned out to be a family physician and his wife a nurse! As the three of us were driving from the railway station to their home, Dr. Tame turned to me and said, "You look very tired. If you don't mind, I'd suggest that you have a nap before supper." I readily agreed. "Sounds great to me." At their charming country cottage, Mrs. Tame ushered me upstairs to a big, airy, attractively furnished bedroom, helped me unpack, and settled me comfortably in the high canopied bed. In a few moments she returned with the traditional "nice cup of tea" and a hot buttermilk scone, lingering only briefly to make sure I had everything I needed. "Just come down when you wake up," she suggested. I fell asleep within minutes of finishing the tea and woke refreshed an hour later, ready for a tasty supper before the fire. However, very soon my eyes began closing again. I was happy to return to my comfortable bed.

The next morning I woke late to bright sunshine streaming through my window and, when I opened the casement, fresh country air and the scent of flowers. It was the middle of March, and this the warmest county in England. Following a breakfast in my room of tea, fried bread and tomatoes, and a real egg, soft-boiled, and then a welcome hot bath, I went downstairs and out into the garden, where Mrs. Tame was at work with a hoe. She had already set out a deck chair for me in the lee of the house, sunny and out of the wind. Cozy under the warm comforter that she had tucked in around me and with a pile of books and magazines on the table beside me, I settled down to a pleasant, restful morning. This was sheer luxury. I already felt much better.

The next day Dr. Tame remarked on how well I looked. "You've made an excellent recovery," he said. "When you arrived, you were on the verge of pneumonia. We were both quite worried." So much for my treatment at the Watford hospital! "Would you like to come with me on my rounds this morning? I think you're well enough, if you'd care to come along. You might like to bring a book and read in the car while I visit my patients."

"Thanks, sounds swell!"

Since Dr. Tame's patients were widely scattered around the countryside, the drive helped orient me to my surroundings, so that on the ensuing days, when he considered me sufficiently recovered to cycle a few miles, I had some idea of where I was going. It was pretty, gently rolling country, only a few miles from the rugged northern coast of Cornwall. The place that intrigued me most, and of which I still have a vivid mind's-eye picture, was Tintagel, legendary site of King Arthur's castle, or one of them. Its rocky promontory jutted precariously out into the choppy sea, waves crashing against the base and throwing up masses of cool salt spray. I stood well back from the edge and breathed the air deeply into my lungs. I felt completely relaxed and at peace for the first time in many months.

The feeling stayed with me the remainder of my nine days' leave with this caring couple, and I returned to London fully recovered physically and in much happier mood. As it turned out, I had been very lucky in taking my leave when I did. The Friday after my return to barracks, Ken phoned to say he was coming up to London for the weekend. He hoped I'd be free, as it would be his last visit "for some time." In a letter to my brother dated April 5, I describe the situation and the weekend:

> With a new order today cancelling all leaves, except for week-end leaves within a fifteen-mile radius, it looks as though I will be getting to know London a little better. I assume Ken must have had advance warning of the order although he didn't say

as much. I managed to get last weekend off even though I was supposed to be on duty.

We decided to make the most of things, with dinner at Kettner's in Soho, Sunday lunch at the Savoy (best food in London, I think), afternoon show at the Tivoli on the Strand (*Jack London*, have you seen it? Really catches the spirit of Jack London's books), and supper at the Chicken Inn, Piccadilly. Seems to me a lot of troops must have known about the cancellation order, because I've never seen the station so crowded as it was on Sunday night. Most likely Ken had to stand all the way back. Certainly glad he was able to get into town, though. He's a darn good kid and I wish him all the luck in the world in what lies ahead. These next few months are likely to be tough for many people.

Although I was enjoying improved health, my social life diminished considerably as a result of the travel restrictions. Work, unrelieved by social distractions, continued dull and totally lacking in challenge. Adding to my frustration was the fact that, although I didn't know much about personnel selection, my superiors knew even less. I was appalled and at times amused by what went on in the department where I spent most of my working time overseas. At one point that spring, it was saddled with the challenging task of selecting paratroop candidates. I would have thought the first thing might have been to enlist the assistance of psychologists. But our one and only psychologist, Major Ferguson, a statistician who would have had considerable knowledge of psychological testing, had by 1944 been posted elsewhere.

The head of the Selection of Personnel Department was a

jolly, breezy sort of fellow. He was also clueless when it came to psychological testing. I've forgotten his name. Let's just call him Colonel X. One day, passing his open office door, I saw the floor littered with papers adorned with colourful splotches of ink or paint. I paused to observe the colonel pick up a paper on his desk, fold it over, and then open it to reveal roughly identical designs on each half. He was attempting to create his own Rorschach (ink blot) test!

Any first-year psychology student would have recognized the absurdity of trying to construct and standardize a test in the few weeks Colonel X had at his disposal. I never did find out whether he actually tried to use this crude, thoroughly unscientific instrument in paratroop selection. In any case, selection might have been more appropriately based on the soldier's past history and an interview by a panel of paratroop officers than on any test then available.

Only once did I date a paratrooper. His is another name that escapes my memory, although I can picture him quite clearly. He had distinguished himself by a noteworthy act of bravery, for which he received a medal. He was a tall, muscular fellow with a lot of vitality and a devil-may-care attitude. Perhaps that's what it took.

We girls were spending many more evenings in barracks at this time, but now and again we dropped into one of the local pubs. One experience stands out. It happened towards the end of May. In a crowded London pub, two young soldiers pushed through the throng to talk to Lil and me. Since they didn't have CANADA patches on their shoulders, we took them for British, until they opened their mouths. Neither could have been more than eighteen, if that. They told us that all identifying insignia had been taken from them. For sure, something big was about to happen. They might not live through it. And so they had gone AWL and come up to London for a last fling.

Not until decades later did I realize the tremendous breach of security being committed. At the time Lil and I felt only sadness at the plight of these two fresh-faced kids, obviously terrified at what lay ahead. I can see their faces even now. Brief though the encounter was, that scene in the pub, their voices, and the hollow feeling in the pit of my stomach remain with me. Until then I had been adventurous and carefree, thinking of little beyond the next leave or the next dance, pushing the war itself far back in my mind, even in the midst of an air raid. Now I couldn't stop thinking about those two kids.

A day or two later, the colonel in charge of the Selection of Personnel Office told me about my new posting. My pleas for a change of job had finally borne fruit. In a few days I would be off to 47 Company, an hour's train ride south of London. After supper that evening, I had just finished relaying the exciting news to my 43 Company roommates when someone called me to the phone. An American sergeant I'd met the previous December was coming into town the next day, a Friday. Would I like to go out? He'd hung around me during our tours at the navigation school, but I hadn't found him particularly interesting.

And so I hesitated a moment before deciding that it might be fun to have one more evening on the town before leaving London. "Be sure to get a weekend pass!" he suggested as he hung up. I had no intention of doing such a thing. One evening with him would be enough. Besides, I wanted to spend most of this last London weekend with my CWAC buddies.

The sergeant picked me up in a cab. That was unusual. My other dates, even Canadian officer friends, always arrived on foot and escorted me to and from our destination on foot or by bus or Underground or a combination of all three. We went to an elegant nightclub, the first I had ever entered in London —or anywhere else, for that matter. My escort and I appeared to be the only uniformed individuals there below the rank of brigadier. I spotted two brigadiers, conspicuous by reason of the red tabs on their lapels, and their ladies at a table on one side of us, and a possible admiral, resplendent in an enormous amount of gold braid, on the other.

I've forgotten the sergeant's name. Let's just call him "Hank." I was slowly and cautiously sipping a second glass of excellent wine when he showed his hand. He told me he'd rented a beautiful suite at Marble Arch and we were about to have one fabulous weekend. He had it all planned out. I was astounded. What arrogance! How presumptuous of him! I couldn't think what I'd done to lead him to assume I'd even consider such a thing. Had someone told him Canadian girls were pushovers? Did some Americans think they were God's gift to women?

I said nothing about my new posting, merely told him I was very sorry, but the orderly room sergeant had refused me a weekend pass, since I'd gone on a couple of cycling weekends with roommates and already used my allotment for the month. This was easier than getting into an argument and risking being left to find my own way back to barracks, although it didn't protect me from a wrestling match in the back of the cab. Fortunately the cabbie, aware of my predicament, drove as fast as blackout conditions permitted and I made my escape in short order.[2]

CHAPTER ELEVEN

SUMMER FUN, MILITARY MUDDLES, BUZZ BOMBS

THE DAY DAWNED bright and beautiful, London's silver-grey barrage balloons floating lazily against the lighter grey high cloud of the sky. Excited about my new posting to the Aldershot-Farnborough area south of London, I hoisted one duffel bag on my shoulder and dragged the other out to the street to await my ride. Minutes later, our commanding officer came running down the steps, shouting, "Filmer-Bennett, we're in France, we're in France!" It was the sixth of June 1944.

The driver and the male officer who had requisitioned the staff car hadn't heard the news. When I broke it to them, at first they thought I was kidding. Once they realized the invasion was under way, they couldn't stop talking, and the three of us chattered excitedly all the way to my destination. Canadian troops had been in the U.K. for four and a half long years, waiting for this moment. For many weeks now, we had known something would be happening soon. The southeast of England had been sealed tight for a couple of months. In spite of those extraordinary security measures, I'm sure the conversation Lil and I had with the two extremely young, frightened Canadian lads in the pub was not an isolated incident. The enemy, too, must have known something would happen before long. However, post-war analyses would later reveal that, despite such minor though worrying breaches of security, our foes had been cleverly deceived as to where and precisely when the invasion would occur. Surprise had been key to the success of D-Day.

My most vivid memory of that historic day is of the late afternoon. Leaning out of my garret window, in one of the century-old row houses of Farnborough's Grant Square, I watched as wave after wave of planes droned overhead on their way back from the Continent. The procession went on for hours. I stopped watching only when the time came to show up at the mess hall for dinner.

It was thanks to Colonel Line, later to become chairman of the Psychology Department at the University of Toronto, that I had finally received a new posting. Rumour had it that he'd been sent over from Canada to see what was wrong with the Selection of Personnel Department. (I could have given him an earful, had I been asked.) Rumour also had it that Colonel Line would be there only two or three weeks. Here was my chance, and I wasn't going to miss it, despite having to go through the "chain of command." I pestered the sergeant major every day until he finally gave in and allowed me to see the visiting VIP. Once through the door of the colonel's office, I found it all a piece of cake, as we used to say. He was instantly sympathetic regarding the plight of an erstwhile psychology student. "I understand," he said. "You want more of a challenge, and you need one." He ordered a reposting, pending a test to ensure I had retained my earlier typing skills. Fortunately I passed the test with ease.

◈

A few days after my arrival at Farnborough's No. 47 Company, I fell victim to the silliest case of army bungling ever. The commanding officer called me into the orderly room. "I'm sorry," she said, "but you weren't given a kit inspection before you left London. Tomorrow morning you'll have to pack up your kit and return to London to have it inspected, reporting back here tomorrow night. Here are your train tickets and meal vouchers. I'm really sorry about this but I have no choice. The order comes from the Area London commander." Kit inspections were mandatory on departure and again on arrival whenever you moved from one company to another, but staff at my previous company had failed to inspect my kit before I left. Despite the fact that my present company had found my kit to be in order, I had to repack, drag my duffel bags onto the train and then through the London Underground, unpack at my old barracks, repack, and then repeat the journey in reverse. All this just so that the missing notation could be inserted into military records! Across the Channel our soldiers were fighting for their lives and ours, and someone at headquarters was fussing about a missing line or two in an unimportant record.

When I sent to Ottawa for my medical records a few years ago, I received a large package of papers containing surprisingly detailed notations covering my entire military career. I was especially amused at the correspondence between the CWAC commander, London Area, the CWAC officers in charge of my London and Farnborough units, and the HQ Department of Personnel Selection. The missed kit inspection was only a small part of that fiasco. The Farnborough CWAC unit hadn't even known I was coming! Luckily they had room for me. It looks as though my London CWAC unit and Personnel Selection both thought it was the other one's responsibility to do the informing. I had fallen through the cracks. Angry missives had gone back and forth. I was the scapegoat in all this. The Area London commander was venting her anger on me, poor defenceless little private.

The Orderly Office of CWAC 47 Company in Farnborough certainly put up a great front. They didn't give the least hint of surprise at my arrival. True, when I look back, the corporal did take my papers into Captain Gough's office and close the door, and it was a good fifteen minutes before the officer came out to meet me. And when the corporal led me to my quarters, the little garret room was completely bare except for a cot. I had to wait for someone to arrive with a chair, sheets, and blankets. However, at the time it didn't occur to me to wonder about that. In the Army, you grew used to accepting many things without question.

I had a glorious summer. Not only had I escaped from Records Office drudgery but also my new locale offered much in the way of extracurricular activity. At HQ CRU (Headquarters, Canadian Reinforcement Units), we young women were in the midst of military camps scattered over many miles in all directions. As in London, the fellows we worked with were mostly older and married, but out at the units we met guys our own age.

Two or three times a week, if we so wished, we could clamber into army trucks taking us to dances at the various camps. We had no shortage of interesting dates, and they were nearby, not as in London available only on leave or the occasional weekend. However, it wasn't merely the social scene that made it a great summer. We could cycle through pleasant, open countryside without first taking a train or cycling miles through city streets to reach it, go punting on the nearby Basingstoke Canal or picnic on its banks. And the air was certainly better than in London.

My new posting had one more advantage, and this a very big one. I found out about it a couple of weeks after my move, when in London for a weekend visit with my old 43 Company roommate, Jeanne. Saturday evening, walking along a street near our YWCA hostel, we heard a steady droning sound in the distance. "Here they are!" Jeanne said. "Those pilotless planes I was telling you about!" Moving rapidly in our direction were four or five of the machines, flying quite low, each with a small light near the front. We stood in a doorway, staring, fascinated. Jeanne explained that we had nothing to fear until the engines cut out. Then these new aerial menaces would coast on in silence for a few seconds before falling to the ground and exploding.

Early the next morning, in our room on the top floor of the hostel, I woke to that same droning sound. Then it stopped, right overhead. I was sure this was the end. My whole life did not flash before my eyes. Neither did I pray to whatever powers may be. I thought, "Here it comes and I forgot to wear my identity discs!" Then, a few seconds later, came the explosion, and the realization that in my drowsy state I'd forgotten that bit about the planes continuing on for a few seconds after the engines cut out. I laughed out loud, waking Jeanne up. How ridiculous, worrying about the identity discs! A direct hit would have smashed both them and me to smithereens.

We gave various names to those instruments of destruction: first they were pilotless planes, then doodlebugs, then buzz bombs, and later v-1s. Their successors, the v-2s, were even scarier. With the v-1s, you were safe as long as you could hear the drone. The best way to protect yourself was to walk or run *towards* the sight and sound of these evil machines. With the v-2s, you had no possible means of protection. You heard nothing until the explosion. v-1s and v-2s were targeted mainly at London, where they killed thousands. Sixty years later, Phyllis told me her heart would still race whenever she heard a siren. Ambulance or fire engine, it made no difference; it still brought back the fear she had experienced in the days of the doodlebugs.[1] I had been posted out of London just in time.

Very shortly after my arrival at 47 Company, I went on my second educational leave. This one took me back to Stratford-upon-Avon for a week-long course of plays, lectures, and social events. I went alone, as I sometimes preferred to do. You met more people that way. Along with a dozen or so other British and Canadian servicewomen, including another CWAC previously unknown to me, I stayed in a Nissen hut. This was a silver-coloured half cylinder of corrugated metal, split lengthwise, the open side resting on a wooden platform. These easily transported and quickly erected structures dotted the countryside. Each provided a long narrow dwelling space under an arched roof, usually—as in this case—furnished with a double row of cots. In the middle, a pot-bellied stove provided reasonable heat, except perhaps in the dead of winter. I remember feeling quite warm and cozy under a couple of standard-issue grey wool blankets.

I loved the intellectual stimulation of that week. Prior to each play, we would attend a preparatory lecture. I believe there were four plays altogether, but I remember and still have the programs for only two: Shakespeare's *A Midsummer Night's Dream* and Ben Jonson's *Volpone*. One day no less a person than Stratford's mayor hosted a luncheon for us at the theatre, attended also by the members of the theatre company. Everyone was very gracious. I must write about this some day, I thought.

The program allowed for a lot of free time for punting on the river and exploring the countryside. Occasionally Cookie, the other CWAC, and I enjoyed the company of three amiable New Zealand Air Force NCOs attached to a nearby RAF bomber unit. Between missions they sought relaxation punting or just drifting down the peaceful Avon. "The river keeps us sane," they said.

I spent most of my last day at Stratford strolling along the banks of the Avon with David, a young RAF sergeant, blond, blue-eyed and utterly charming. We parted at the railway station with a good-bye hug, hopes of meeting sometime at his

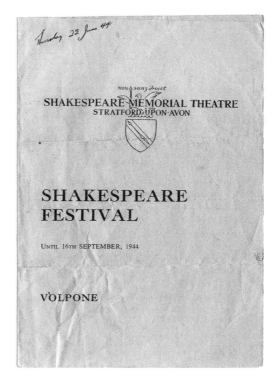

Memento of a memorable
leave at Stratford.

family home in Wales, and a promise to write, a promise we
were to continue keeping for some time.

Summer and fall at 47 Company were close to perfect.
While my job was far from challenging, at least I was allowed
not only to type letters and reports but also, often, to compose
them myself. Amazing!

Three or four weeks after my arrival in Farnborough, I was
delighted to hear from Trev. He had, with some difficulty,

managed to track me down. Since his posting was close by, we were able to spend many a pleasant Saturday or Sunday together, strolling along the banks of the Basingstoke Canal or sometimes taking the train to London for the day, when we would invariably go to a movie or, more likely, a play. I saw Trev on most weekends, but I went out on dates or to dances several nights during the week.

We girls would dance every dance, with no shortage of partners. I still love the music of that era, particularly that of Glenn Miller and the songs made famous by Vera Lynn.[2] There is nothing like music to take one back.

Occasionally one or another of us would go on leave with a male friend. I did that only once, with a young man named Tommy, when he and I went to Edinburgh that September. No *True Confessions* magazine stuff, however! We stayed in separate homes, a few blocks apart. We girls tended to be very proper in those days. Anyway, Tommy was a couple of years my junior, and at that age two years seemed a lot. His personnel record had suggested an unusually high intelligence rating, and he was indeed an interesting companion. He had an incredible memory as well as a sparkling wit. He wasn't handsome, being bespectacled and what today might be called "nerdy-looking," but I had always valued temperament and intelligence above looks, and in both he rated more highly than most of the other men I dated. Almost always in a happy mood, he was a delightful conversationalist.

Why I chose to go to Scotland again, after that February 1943 experience in freezing-cold Aberdeen, I have absolutely no idea. September weather in Edinburgh was almost as ghastly: less windy and a littler warmer, but even wetter. Still,

Tommy and I tramped the city streets every day. I remember climbing the big hill to the castle in pouring rain, only to find the building closed, and then hurrying down past the Walter Scott Monument and along Princes Street in search of a comfortable pub where we could have a hot toddy and dry off. We were lucky to find one with a cozy fireplace nook. That week we checked out a few pubs, visited a museum, saw several movies, and hung out in a British canteen. We enjoyed each other's company and talked non-stop. After that trip, however, our dates became fewer and farther apart. I was sorry, but with no shortage of other dates, only mildly so. It didn't occur to me at the time, but I suspect Tommy had hoped for more from our little jaunt. I had missed a number of small clues, things a more perceptive young woman might have picked up on.

I grew up a lot during those overseas years, as we all did in the Corps. We were mostly very young, and for many this was our first experience away from home. For a very few girls (say, three out of one hundred), and not always just the younger ones, the experience ended unhappily, with an unexpected pregnancy. In that era before the pill, the risk was significant and the stigma great. Most of these young women truly believed themselves engaged, and it was a shock to discover in all too many cases that the supposed "fiancé" had a wife back in Canada or the USA. An orderly room sergeant told me of one case where CWAC officers confronted the man and insisted that he marry the girl. "I wish I could," he said, "but I have a wife and two kids back in Canada."

Girls so "caught" often did everything possible to hide their condition. If they hid it long enough, it would be too late for them to be shipped home in disgrace. Instead, they could have the baby in the U.K. and have it adopted there. The event still meant discharge from the service, but at least the girl would be saved the shame of arriving home pregnant. When she did reach home, no doubt she would make up some cover story to satisfy the family, or at least the neighbours. One CWAC, who had come over on an early draft and who kept her baby, claimed to have been secretly married before leaving Canada, to an American airman since killed in combat. The airman had been a first cousin with a surname the same as hers, she said, and so her name had not changed on marriage. The nursing sisters at the hospital believed her, or at least put on a good show of doing so, addressing her as "Mrs. Evans," but many of her colleagues did not accept her story. I suspended judgement. Anyway, it was none of my business.[3]

In her book *We Never Stopped Dancing,* Nano Pennefather-McConnell treats this subject with great compassion. Given the heavy responsibility of supervising young airwomen in this predicament, arranging for their journey home or care during and after delivery, as well as care of the baby, she felt their suffering deeply and deplores the harshness with which they were often judged. At one point, she describes the experience of a young airwoman who went AWL for several weeks, until the ship on which she was to be sent home had already sailed and her pregnancy had advanced to the point where it would be unsafe to send her home under wartime conditions. This presented the Air Force Command with a dilemma. Normally missing one's ship warranted a charge of desertion and a court martial. The girl was brought up on charge, but there was no precedent and no fitting penalty for the "crime." She was finally "confined to barracks," except that the Air Force girls had no barracks. They lived out. And so she was put in the custody of three sergeants, living with them and accompanying them everywhere they went until she went to the hospital to have her baby. This and other such sad situations affected Nano deeply, and likely had much to do with her post-war career choice of social work.

One evening in the fall of '44, we girls of 47 Company were ordered to put on our pyjamas and line up in our square outside and up the stairs to the nurse's office. (We lived in row houses on two sides of Grant Square, with the orderly room, other offices, and a gate taking up a third side. The fourth, securely fenced, backed onto an empty field.) The idea of a pyjama parade puzzled us, but we had to follow orders unquestioningly. One by one, girls entered the office. Margaret, just ahead of me, came storming out, face red with anger as she stomped down the stairs and back across the square to her quarters. Then it was my turn to lie on the table and have my stomach prodded by a nurse and a doctor who looked hardly old enough to have graduated from medical school. We weren't given any explanation, and only Margaret had dared request one.

Later she told us what happened. When she asked, "What's this all about?" the smart-aleck young medical officer responded, with a leer, "Just come over to my office some evening and I'll show you what it's all about!" Risking a charge of insubordination, she shot back, "How dare you talk to me that way! I'll have you know I'm a respectable married woman with an eighteen-year-old daughter." Margaret was thirty-six. Both she and her daughter Pat had enlisted in England that spring. I had already come to know Pat at 43 Company.

Much later Millie, our sergeant major, told a couple of us what had led up to this undignified procedure: "We had to go through all that nonsense because earlier in the year, two or three girls in London hid their pregnancies until it was too late to ship them home. But that nasty little medical officer didn't discover anything here. Captain Gough and I were plenty relieved, I can tell you!"

I doubt you will find details like this in the official accounts. One of my army pals who was with me on that infamous "pyjama parade" never mentioned it again, and she quickly changed the subject when many years later I alluded to it in the presence of several mutual friends. At one of our CWAC reunions, when we were all asked to fill out a lengthy questionnaire concerning army experiences, I included the pyjama parade story along with several other anecdotes. All my stories later appeared in *Athene*, a history of the Corps, but the exchange between the brash young doctor and Margaret had been cut.

In a similar vein, I've never heard or read any reference to the disastrous and thankfully aborted rope-descending exercise at 43 Company, but then I have never taken the trouble to plunge into the archives. This is simply an account of my war as I remember it. There may be some CWAC veterans still living who recall these or similar unfortunate incidents. Perhaps it is out of loyalty to the military and to the Corps that such things are seldom mentioned.

CHAPTER TWELVE

FLYING HATS AND FABULOUS COFFEE

Two weeks after my arrival at 47 Company, I acquired a roommate. When you have just one roommate, she had better be the right one. Sunny, my roommate at 47 Company, proved to be a good pal.

With the added military activity, our office workload increased to the point where we had to increase our staff. I enjoyed supervising Aileen and Cay, the two new clerks, under the direction of our kindly staff sergeant boss. Jim, who had been a registered nurse in civilian life, was a soft-spoken gentle man who treated us with great consideration. If you made some silly mistake, he would make sure no one was within earshot when he drew your attention to it. An excellent administrator, he'd inevitably end his little chat with a word of encouragement. We all appreciated such unusual sensitivity and in consequence put extra effort into our work.

Happy at work, I also enjoyed barracks living and a busy social life. The gate to Grant Square was never locked or even closed. In fact, now that I think about it, I'm not even sure there was a gate. When going out in the evening, we were supposed to check out via the orderly room, beside the entrance, and to check in on our return. However, if you failed to check out, you had no problem slipping in even quite late at night, there being no record you had ever gone out. I developed the habit of skipping the checking process at times, particularly if I were going some distance and might have difficulty getting back before the eleven o'clock curfew. Just after midnight on one such evening, I was walking briskly along the pavement towards my house, close to the end of the row, when a voice hollered out from a top-floor window, "Who's there?"

"Just me," I responded cheerily, then doubled my pace until reaching my door, dashed up the two flights of stairs with all possible speed, and stumbled into the garret room. "Somebody's after me," I called to Sunny as I tossed my hat on the shelf and dived, fully clothed even to shoes, under the covers of my cot. Almost immediately we heard the door open below and the duty sergeant ask, "Did someone just come through here?" The girls on the first floor denied hearing a thing, bless their hearts, as did those on the second. Meanwhile I had begun breathing heavily in what I hoped was a good imitation of a sound sleeper. Up came my pursuer. "Did someone just come in here?" I continued my act, while Sunny played the part of someone being slowly aroused from a deep sleep. She turned over, gave a kind of groan, and murmured a faint "Wha—wha—at?" The duty sergeant repeated the question, whereupon Sunny muttered a few barely intelligible words of denial and snuggled back into her pillow. At this point I rolled over, breathing harder than ever. The sergeant left, but Sunny and I took the precaution of maintaining silence. I don't remember whether or not I slept the entire night in my clothes. I may have.

A few weeks later, my name came up for promotion. A common process, one favoured by our commanding officer, was to grant one stripe at a time. First you were a lance corporal, then after a couple of months, assuming good behaviour, you became a corporal, after which you could hope in due course to be awarded a third stripe and attain the lofty status of sergeant. Sunny, who was gorgeous and glamorous and had only to flutter her eyelashes to have men falling at her feet, happened to be working in the office that dealt with promotions. She had no difficulty whatsoever in persuading the male officers to give me two stripes right off the bat and then a third within the shortest allowable time after that. Before October ended, I was a sergeant. I heard via the grapevine that our commanding officer was not especially pleased. Looking back, I can't say I blame her.

I was far from an exemplary soldier, as was well demonstrated on the parade ground one day shortly after my arrival in Farnborough. In London we had seldom done any marching, other than on church parades, from which I was eventually released because of my flat feet. Our Farnborough officers had not been fussing about drill either, but suddenly visiting brass decided we should march aimlessly up and down the parade ground every Friday afternoon. All went smoothly enough until one Friday when a sudden gust of wind sent my hat sailing through the air. Being in the last row of the platoon, where it was easy to slip out of line, I dashed off in hot pursuit. Alas, every time I went to grab my hat, another gust of wind carried it farther, until I ended up at the opposite end of the parade ground. I could hear some shouting in the distance, but could not make out the words. I plunked the hat back on my unruly mop of hair and ran to resume my place in the platoon, neatly falling into step. "Halt!" hollered the sergeant major. "Just where did you take your basic training?" she demanded. "I didn't, ma'am," I replied.

That was another case of army bungling, but one for which I was grateful. The rules required that new recruits be sent for six weeks of basic training at special camps set up for the purpose. I'd heard the training was quite gruelling and was glad someone had slipped up, and even put me on overseas draft without noticing that omission in my records. Millie, the sergeant major, wasn't the tyrant her rank might suggest, but rather a very sweet, gentle person, who calmly explained that you never, ever break ranks, no matter what piece of your equipment might fall off. Now I understood why that girl marching in London had just stepped out of her army-issue panties and kept going when the button gave way.

Slacks would have been far preferable to skirts, if merely because of the unreliable panties. In Canada and the U.K., only drivers were permitted to wear battledress, and then only when doing the weekly vehicle maintenance.[1] Practicality also won out over tradition for those girls landing on the Continent before VE Day, who sometimes had to cope with primitive conditions. Otherwise the rules were very strict. Sixty years after the fact, one of my friends still complained bitterly about a male medical officer in the hospital where she was convalescing after suffering a knee injury. He refused permission for slacks even during therapeutic exercises that required her to elevate her legs to a point exposing garters and a large expanse of hideous orange to all and sundry.

Despite my poor performance on the parade ground, I was performing well in the Selection of Personnel Office and looked forward to the prospect of further promotion. I was therefore greatly disappointed when Jim, our pleasant staff sergeant boss, was posted elsewhere, and I, next in line for the job, was passed over in favour of a CWAC sergeant from London. Major Brewer, an officer being posted to our unit, had arranged to bring this outsider down with him. They came from the same hometown in New Brunswick. Although I kept my disappointment to myself, Aileen and Cay must have sensed and shared it, because Gen, the newcomer, later commented on how coolly she had been received by her staff. She turned out to be a lovely person, liked by us all, who became my lifelong friend. I never had the heart to admit to the initial coolness, let alone the reason for it.

Sunny was also supportive during this time. Although she was a great roommate, I didn't habitually hang out with her. It would have been too hard on the ego. Few if any of the rest of us in 47 Company could hold our own with an Elizabeth Taylor look-alike. When Sunny was on the scene, the guys had eyes for no one else. One weekend, however, when Trev was away on manoeuvres, the two of us did go on a jaunt to the Portsmouth-Southampton area. The autumn weather was perfect—clear and warm.

Saturday afternoon we had decided to visit Nelson's flagship the H M S *Victory*, resting at its age-old berth in a dockyard now crowded with Allied naval vessels. Being in uniform, we had no difficulty getting in. The fellow in the guardhouse simply noted our names and regimental numbers, pointed out the route to the *Victory*, and sent us on our way. At the foot of the ship's gangplank stood a portly gentleman in old-style naval garb. In a capricious mood not unusual for her, Sunny smiled her dazzling smile and gushed, "Are you Mr. Nelson?"

"Oh no, my dear," the chap replied, very solemnly, "he died some one hundred and fifty years ago." Since I'd forgotten much of what I'd learned in school about Horatio Nelson and the Battle of Trafalgar, and Sunny had forgotten even more than I, we found the half-hour tour interesting enough. However, the rest of the afternoon proved much more fun.

Sauntering along the dock, we came to an American ship, a good part of whose crew was lounging on the prow, basking in the sun. One glance from my gorgeous pal and they invited us on board. A courteous bunch of fellows, they gave us a tour of their ship and then tall glasses of pure grapefruit juice, chocolate cake with real icing and steaming cups of Chase and Sanborn coffee. Not only that, but on our way through the galley, where our eyes had bugged out at the sight of a pile of hard-boiled eggs, sliced in half in preparation for devilling, they filched a couple of those for us. We had not seen such food in almost two years. And so we spent a delightful afternoon chatting with our new-found friends and enjoying their hospitality.

Finally, after a couple of hours, we thanked our hosts and

headed back to the guardhouse. Little did we know what reception would await us there.

The guard glared at us. "Where have you girls been?" he roared. "We've been looking all over the shipyard for you. You should have been back here two hours ago!" Sunny did her best with the dazzling smile and fluttering of eyelashes, but that didn't work with this guy. "Our men have been searching for you for over an hour!" he bellowed. "Just where were you?"

"You didn't give us a deadline when we came in, and anyway your men couldn't have looked very hard," said Sunny sweetly. "We were sitting on the prow of an American ship in full view." This had the effect of applying a match to a powder keg. We just stood there meekly until the blaze fizzled out. Finally dismissed, we marched smartly away, grateful to have avoided ending up in the brig or wherever the Navy tosses its delinquents.

A few years ago, my old high school friend Nellie told me about her husband Harold's experience that same year on a Canadian ship anchored next to an American one similar to the one Sunny and I visited. For all I know this could have happened in the same shipyard. For weeks the Canadian sailors endured the tantalizing odour of ham and real eggs and Chase and Sanborn coffee wafting over from the American ship, while they themselves sat down to powdered-egg concoctions and chicory-laced third-rate coffee. Finally they could stand it no longer. There must have been collusion with one or more sailors on the American ship, but somehow the Canadians managed to steal a whole ham and several dozen eggs plus a quantity of coffee. At that time, Harold, a commercial fisherman in civilian life, was filling in for the regular cook, who was on leave. When the next morning the captain sat down to a breakfast of ham and eggs and excellent coffee, he asked Harold where this feast had come from. Harold said something like, "Ask me no questions, sir, and I'll tell you no lies." The good food was too much for the captain to resist. He asked no questions and ate up.

At about the same time, the American captain was gazing with dismay at his meagre breakfast: a solitary egg and one miserably thin slice of ham. "Shortage of supplies, sir," his cook explained. Suspicions aroused, the American captain accosted his Canadian counterpart, demanding that the latter's ship be searched. The Canadian welcomed him aboard, secure in the knowledge that the evidence had been eaten and drunk, and any telltale signs of the crime, like eggshells, carefully hidden by his efficient, well-trained crew. He trusted his men implicitly. Justly proud of them and his immaculate ship, he delighted in showing the American captain around. To top off the visit, he then treated his guest to a cup of steaming, chicory-laced coffee.

CHAPTER THIRTEEN

MORE THAN ONE
KIND OF WOUND

M Y BUSY SOCIAL LIFE continued well into late fall, with little change until the increasing number of casualties on the Continent began emptying the reinforcement units of their complement of men, to be replaced by fresh young recruits from Canada. These replacements would stay only a month or two before also shipping out across the Channel. Life became uncertain, depressing, harrowing. We carried on as usual, but the war weighed more and more heavily on our minds.

All summer I had been worrying about Ken. We had remained good pals and a constant in each other's lives over the past couple of years. I could usually count on a brief letter every two or three weeks, yet I hadn't had a word since that early-April weekend in London. And so it was a great relief one morning to see Ken's handwriting on a card bearing an English postmark. He had been wounded, though "not badly," and shipped back from the Continent to a hospital about an hour's travel from HQ CRU.

The next day I dashed off after work and headed for that hospital by train and bike, forgoing dinner. When I did reach the place, I had to muster up every bit of courage and persuasive power I possessed to gain entry. They didn't normally allow visitors during the week. I wrote to my brother: "You should have seen Ken's face when I walked into the ward. So overcome with surprise and delight, he almost leaped out of bed. Luckily he's come off pretty light, gun shot in the leg, says shouldn't keep him laid up more than a couple of months. He certainly looks well."

A fortnight later, after his move to a convalescent hospital closer to HQ CRU, I visited Ken again. Early on a sunny Saturday afternoon I set off on the half-hour bus ride. I was happy to see him and his three ward mates on their hospital beds outdoors, under the shade of huge umbrellas. They all looked well and seemed in good spirits. Ken was still in a cast, but expected to be out of it in two or three weeks. We enjoyed a pleasant few hours, sharing anecdotes and sometimes chatting with ambulatory patients strolling around the grounds. A nurse brought tea mid-afternoon and stayed to chat a while. She and one of the fellows hailed from the same small town in Saskatchewan. Around five an orderly came with supper for the men and for me as well. Some hundred yards away, buses came and went at half-hour intervals, stopping only two or three minutes to drop off and pick up passengers. On my arrival I had announced my intention of catching the six-thirty, to get back in time for a seven o'clock date.

I saw my bus arriving. I gave Ken a hug, wished everyone well, and prepared to leave. He gripped my arm firmly. I tried to pull away. He tightened his grip. One of his fellow patients ordered, "For God's sake, let her go!" He hung on. The men swore at him. "But she's going out with another guy," he protested. "So?" yelled the guy in the next bed. "Don't be a prick!" I was almost in tears. "You're hurting me," I complained. This nonsense went on for the best part of five minutes. The bus was going to leave without me.

I yanked with all my might, even though that made my arm hurt more. The fellow in the farthest bed pushed himself up on his elbows and thundered, "Let her go! That's an order, *lieutenant!*" Abruptly, Ken released his grip. I fell back, almost losing my balance. "Okay, leave!" he muttered, almost inaudibly. Who was he, to pull rank on me? I was not going to run madly down the road at his bidding, only to have the bus drive off before I reached it. "No," I said, "I don't feel in the mood for running. I'm just going to sit here another half-hour, well out of reach, while I chat with these three *gentlemen*."

The three gentlemen looked extremely uncomfortable. Ken glowered. No one could think of anything to say, although a couple of the fellows made a desultory attempt to lighten the atmosphere by talking about the previous evening's entertainment. The conversation fizzled out. I felt bad. I wasn't being fair to the other three men. God knows what they had all been through, across the Channel. I said goodbye again, wished everyone, including Ken, a speedy recovery, and went off to await the next bus.

That incident upset me deeply. I had lost a trusted friend and confidant. I was not happy to find out he'd turned into a jealous swain, especially one with a propensity for violence. As time went on, I thought more and more about Trev. He remained the kindest, dearest fellow I had yet met. I particularly recall one October Sunday. We had taken a train to London and then a bus about twenty miles north to historic St. Albans, where my mother had lived for several years during her childhood. I wanted to see the town for that reason, but also for its Roman ruins. Unfortunately, in the midst of our explorations the weather turned foul. We were pretty well soaked by the time we found shelter in a delightful little pub. We had the place to ourselves. The jovial, kindly landlady made a great fuss over us, taking our sopping coats and hanging them to one side of the fire, ushering us over to a comfortable sofa in front of it, and quickly heating some scones in the oven to go with our tea. We must have sat there a couple of hours, sharing thoughts and feelings to a greater extent than we had ever done before. It was the one and only time we ever held hands. Neither of us wanted to leave. But we had to get back to London in time for the train that would take us to our respective barracks. Reluctantly, we dragged ourselves out of that warm cocoon into the cold teeming rain.

The next Saturday Trev seemed quieter than usual. I asked if anything was wrong.

"Well," he said, "I don't know. I just don't know. A few weeks ago I sent Fern flowers for her birthday."

"You haven't heard since? Sometimes the mail's pretty slow."

"Oh, she wrote and thanked me. The letter came yesterday. It was dated two weeks after she got the flowers."

A London day ticket. Note the phrase "in uniform,"
one reason I usually wore mine even on leave.

"Maybe she made a mistake with the date."

"It was the same as the postmark on the envelope."

I didn't know what to say. Why the delay? "Maybe she'd
been ill or something happened she didn't want to worry you
about."

Trev smiled and hugged me warmly. "Nice try, Doris. You
are a sweetheart."

How ironic, I thought, if while we had been keeping tight
control of our feelings, his wife back home was carrying on
with someone else. But I kept that thought to myself. I suggested we go to the local cinema to see *Melody Inn*, with
Dorothy Lamour and Dick Powell. I hoped a light-hearted
musical might lift Trev's spirits a little.

During the ensuing weeks, my dear friend was able to get over less often. The cadet program was nearing a close. When he did manage a visit he treated me especially warmly, but said nothing further about his wife and I hesitated to ask. Our final rendezvous came towards the end of November. I sensed this would be the last before he shipped out. He could not say, of course. But he didn't need to. If his manner, quiet and wistful, more serious than usual, had not relayed the message, the goodbye bear hug would have. We clung tightly to each other, neither wanting to let go. I fought back the tears. Would I ever see him again?

A week later my leave came due. I had chosen to stay, under the hospitality scheme, with an elderly couple in Falmouth, Cornwall, where the weather might be tolerable. Although we did have a couple of days of watery sun, the air was always distinctly chilly, the huge house one giant icebox. I would have been warmer staying in barracks, at least in my office and the sergeants' mess with their pot-bellied stoves. My obviously well-to-do hosts had sufficient fuel only for the tiny fireplace in the den. We all huddled together there during the day, conversing and reading and just relaxing, except at mealtimes. For ten minutes before each meal, a small electric heater near one end of the long table took a tiny edge off the chill in the enormous dining room. I wore one of my kind host's heavy hand-knit sweaters over my army-issue wool pullover and, with his wife's shawl over my knees, ate as quickly as etiquette allowed. We then hurried back into the warmth of the den, or on occasion emerged from the icebox for a brisk walk around town. We were sometimes warmer outdoors. I could not help thinking back to my first overseas leave. The spinsters in their humble Aberdeen cottage lived more comfortably than my Falmouth hosts in their lavishly furnished mansion. Wartime austerity was a great leveller.

Several days I went exploring on my own, bundled up in my heavy greatcoat, army-issue wool scarf doubled around my neck. One sunny day I took the ferry across what my host told me was "the world's third-largest natural harbour" to St. Mawes, a picturesque small town about a mile away. I would have liked to tour its castle, less than a mile from the ferry dock, but, when told the building was closed for the duration, decided the climb was not worth the bother. And so, as was my wont on Falmouth excursions, I whiled away the afternoon in a quaint little tea shop, munching on warm baking-powder biscuits and sipping piping-hot tea. By this time I had come to share the Britisher's delight in "a nice cup of tea," remedy for whatever ails.

I dreaded the climb to my icy bedroom at night, the decor as daunting as the temperature. As I ascended the wide staircase into ever colder air, I looked straight into the jaws of a lion. Never had I seen such a rug! I then hurried down the broad hallway under the eyes of tigers, leopards and other jungle creatures, whose heads jutted out from the walls on either side. I lost no time in escaping their scrutiny and clambering into the high four-poster canopied bed, undressing beneath the pile of blankets, all my clothes tucked snugly in with me. A wrinkled uniform concerned me not at all. I'd press it when I got back to barracks.

The gloomy weather and unrelenting cold did little to lift my spirits. I had been unable to forget the disastrous encounter with Ken at the hospital. Worse still, I kept thinking about

Trev. As was my habit when feeling low, I took refuge in books, particularly books of poetry, especially the copy of *The Rubaiyat of Omar Khayyam* Trev had given me for my birthday. I read it over and over until I knew every word by heart. That volume lies open before me now, Trev's birthday wishes and signature on the flyleaf.

∽

On my return to barracks, I found a letter from Ken. He was starting a fourteen-day leave. Would I go up to London with him the next weekend? I was wary. Where was the apology for his appalling behaviour? Was he waiting to deliver it in person, or did it not occur to him that he owed me one? I wrote back that I was already planning a London weekend with my friend Millie, the CWAC sergeant major. If he produced an escort for her, we might all go together. And then I ran across the square to Millie's quarters.

"Millie, how about going to London with me and a couple of good-looking Canadian officers next weekend? They'll stay at a service club and I can wangle accommodation for us at 43 Company."

Millie hesitated. Pretty but reserved in manner, she socialized little. "Come on, they'll take us dancing at the

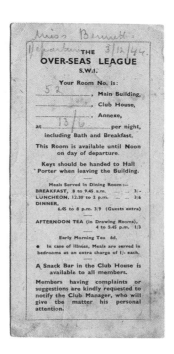

The Over-Seas League service club was reasonably comfortable and conveniently located.

Wellington Club, and Ken promises dinner at Claridge's. You've got to come!"

And so she did. The four of us enjoyed a great weekend, although we dined at an exclusive nightclub, the Bagatelle, rather than the promised Claridge's. Only many years later when I read about this club being a favourite haunt of Princess Margaret and her friends did I realize just how exclusive it must have been. At the time, I was less impressed with my posh surroundings than with the food. For the first and last time in my life, I enjoyed the intriguing though slightly fishy taste of an enormous seagull's egg. It was almost like old times with Ken, except that the hospital incident kept popping into the back of my mind. He acted as though nothing had happened. I let it go. In two or three weeks, this man would be heading back into battle. Who knew whether he would survive a second time?

Christmas was rapidly approaching. Our officers made an effort to create a cheery atmosphere in the newly opened CWAC recreation hut. With the onset of winter and continuing gloomy news from across the Channel, morale needed boosting. The officers and senior NCOs scrounged material from quartermaster stores for decorations, hunted up sheet music for the piano, and encouraged the girls to hang out together during the evenings instead of retreating to barrack rooms. Singsongs became popular. We didn't know anything about music therapy in those days, but I for one felt my spirits lifted after an evening belting out popular ditties and our favourite marching songs. We needed music and we needed each other.

Christmas parcels began arriving. We girls shared the contents. Our Selection of Personnel Office developed a festive air as officers there shared their own treats with us. I particularly appreciated Major Brewer's offering of Christmas cake. My mother had sent one but, alas, it arrived reeking of fire retardant. I never could bear to tell her.

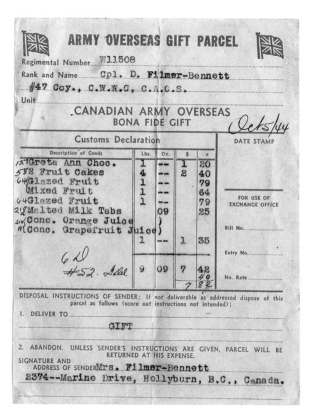

A listing of contents in an overseas
gift parcel from my mother.

We ate well on Christmas Day: *two* boiled eggs and a slice of ham for breakfast, and at dinner the traditional turkey with all the trimmings. The next evening, Ken and Bob (Millie's London date) invited the two of us to their mess at Aldershot.

Our only problem had been deciding what to wear. We other ranks could not advertise our lowly status by wearing our uniforms in the officers' mess. Technically officers were not supposed to be fraternizing with us, although outside of the mess no one paid the slightest attention to that rule. Our civilian wardrobes were severely limited, but as usual in such cases we girls all borrowed from fellow CWACs. In this way Millie and I came up with attire that compared favourably with that worn by the civilian guests, their wardrobes severely restricted by years of rationing. Ken and Bob entertained us royally, the feast proving even more sumptuous than expected.

I had a particularly good time that evening. Although Ken appeared fully recovered, he danced less than usual. That allowed me a greater variety of partners, including his commanding officer. "I remember you from our New Year's Eve dance last year," the man said as he approached me. "We didn't get to dance then. How's about making up for that now?" I was grateful this man hadn't asked me to dance last year, when I was still stumbling over my partner's feet. I would never be a good dancer, but the past few months of frequenting reinforcement unit dances had provided enough practice to make me a passable one.

"I remember you," the commanding officer said, as we danced away, "because you were the only girl wearing a strapless evening gown[1] and also the only redhead. You have gorgeous hair."

That was the first compliment I'd ever received about my hair. Although a pretty shade, coppery with natural highlights, it was also unduly thick and difficult to manage, sometimes resembling "a broom bush in a fit" according to my mother. I must have managed to tame it more than usual that evening.

On New Year's Eve, I enjoyed still another wonderful feast, this time in our sergeants' mess. We ate our way through five courses: hors d'oeuvres, soup with fancy rolls, turkey with its usual accompaniments, mince pie and plum pudding, cheese and crackers. All that festivity and good food boosted my spirits, at least for a few days.

CHAPTER FOURTEEN

WINTER CHILLS

CHRISTMAS HAD COME and gone. Lots of replacements came and went, too, but I determined to avoid becoming attached to anyone. The war machine would soon get these men in its clutches and toss them into the horror across the Channel.

With all the troop movements, our office work increased. More and more letters had to be typed, reports filed, telephone queries answered. In addition, there were more "Cook's Tours," our term for the arrival of visiting brass from CMHQ. I had no idea why these VIPs turned up so often. They always disappeared into the inner office to confer with our two officers; we clerks were not privy to their discussions.

One day while busily typing I looked up at the broad khaki-clad back of a man perched on a corner of my small desk.

Taking him to be the driver awaiting his elite passengers, I announced firmly, in my best sergeant's voice: "In this office we do not sit on the desks." The man sprang up and turned to face me, smiling pleasantly. "Oh, pardon me, sergeant. I do apologize." I gaped at the bright-red tabs adorning his lapels. I had ordered a brigadier to get his butt off my desk! My throat went dry, but I recovered enough to stammer, "Apology gratefully accepted, sir."

January 1945 was extremely cold. My garret room, no longer cheered by the presence of Sunny, who had been granted her wish for transfer to *The Army Show*,[1] was unheated except for whatever faint warmth could be coaxed from its tiny, shallow fireplace. The coal bin on the landing outside the door held only black dust with an occasional minuscule lump of coal. If by using some scraps of paper and a few sticks of kindling I did manage to get a fire started, the only way to keep it going was to make a bellows out of a piece of stiff cardboard, if available. More often than not I succeeded only in scorching the cardboard and the fire died out. I usually gave up in disgust and more than once slept in almost all the clothing I possessed, under the two army-issue blankets and my greatcoat.

The other eight girls in the house—four on the first floor, four on the second—stayed a little warmer, though at a price. The rooms they shared were adjacent to kitchens equipped with a small shilling-fed gas heater. Nevertheless, my trips to the second-floor toilet, reached by traversing the sleeping room, unused kitchen, and then an icy corridor housing the bath, were decidedly chilly. One morning I observed in horror an immense icicle hanging from the bathtub tap. We didn't take many baths that month. To tell the truth, I don't remember ever seeing an occupant in that tub as I passed on my way to the toilet, or using it much myself. I suspect we must have made do with sponge baths for the most part.

The men of HQ CRU fared better for warmth, if not privacy. They lived in long brick huts, each housing maybe ten or a dozen fellows and heated by a large, centrally located pot-bellied stove. Non-commissioned officers, at least those above the rank of corporal, enjoyed greater privacy, in huts divided into double or sometimes single rooms.

Like all the other HQ CRU offices, the Selection of Personnel Office was in one of those rectangular huts. With a pot-bellied stove all to ourselves at one end of the building, we were warmer at work than in our own quarters. The coziest hut of all was the sergeants' mess. Featuring a bar, lounge, dining room and kitchen, it was our country club—a place to sit and relax, read the scandalous Sunday *News of the World*,[2] eat, and socialize, the best perk that had come along with the third stripe on my sleeve last October. Frequently we held our own dances. The most important feature, which I appreciated on a daily basis, was the dining room, where we were served at the table. Not since late fall had I been required to line up at the cookhouse and wash my own dishes. I had really come up in the world!

Younger than the male sergeants, we half-dozen CWACS brought to the dances young men stationed at the various field units in the area. Apart from being too old for us, the HQ CRU sergeants were mostly far from attractive.[3] The nicest, a genuinely fine person with a rollicking sense of humour, was Andy Beck, our pay sergeant. I never went out with Andy—no one did—but we kidded around a great deal. He was a very good-looking fellow with dark hair and twinkling black eyes. Like most of the others, he was married, but unlike many of them, he was absolutely true-blue to his wife back home. I admired him for that. It seemed a rare quality.

With a few notable exceptions, the remaining sergeants were an odd lot. I never could understand what their English girlfriends saw in them. There was one I hated to sit opposite when dining. This fellow ate his meals on the double, quick-marching his way through the rubbery dehydrated potatoes, the grainy-textured, crumbly liver some said had been too long frozen, even the half-cooked boiled rice pudding, which I habitually abandoned after first extracting the few raisins tossed in with it. (The quality of our food, which had always been surprisingly good considering the circumstances, deteriorated markedly in the early months of 1945.) The worst place to be was in the seat directly opposite this oaf, because then you were right in the line of fire. It was enough to face this unpalatable stuff every day, without having to view it in his gaping mouth and fight off the barrage of moist morsels spewing out along with a steady stream of food-muffled words.

Another unsavoury character I privately called yellow-tooth Wally. His teeth and fingers stained with nicotine, he presided over the bar, leering at us young women and dispensing liquor and safes and dirty jokes. And then there was Bill, the horribly old staff sergeant with the enormous pot belly. I never saw these men doing any kind of drill, which might have helped to keep them fit. Presumably involved in some kind of sedentary work, they sat around in their spare time and drank beer and consorted with English women living in the area. Some of those women were very likeable, too good for these slobs. I felt sorry for them. They would soon be left high and dry when the men went back to their wives and families in Canada.

Despite the improvement in my status, that winter comes to mind as generally drab and dreary. Dances at the various reinforcement units were less fun than formerly. Fellows I had met over the previous few months were off across the Channel, their replacements appallingly young, and soon on their way in any case. The rapid turnover of personnel was depressing, not only because you never had a chance to get to know anyone, but also because of its obvious significance: casualties were increasing and replacements were being rushed to fill the gaps.[4]

One of those young men still vivid in memory was a tall, good-looking fellow with a mop of dark, curly hair, who had enlisted after a couple of years at the University of Manitoba. Charlie and I were instantly drawn to each other, but I was still worrying about Ken and Trev, and I had earlier vowed not to become attached to anyone. In any case, our time together was brief. Seven or eight dates over a few weeks, and then one evening he arrived loaded with small packages. This would be our last evening, he told me, and I might as well have the remains of his recent parcel from home. I left the gifts in a secure spot in the orderly room while we walked into Aldershot to a favourite pub, chatted by the fire, and then strolled slowly back. I hugged Charlie a reluctant goodbye. The next evening I shared his four-pound box of chocolates with fellow CWACs in the recreation hut, the treats bittersweet.

Chance plays a huge part in our lives. Given more time, I could easily have fallen in love with Charlie, or even perhaps with David, the Welsh lad I met in Stratford and with whom I was still corresponding. David and I had tried several times to meet on leave, but the war always got in the way. And now I'd had to say goodbye to Charlie. I wondered if I would ever see either of them again.

February came, and still no word from Trev. Unfortunately, HQ CRU did not keep records of men once they left the reinforcement area, and I no longer knew anyone working at CMHQ Records. From time to time I ran across men from the cadet training centre. None had known Trev. Then, one gloomy February day, I almost whooped with joy on seeing the familiar handwriting on a soiled, crumpled envelope with a U.K. postmark. I tore it open eagerly.

The brief note was dated December 15. Trev wrote: "I'm giving this to a friend to mail. Can't write more now, just wishing you a happy Christmas. Take care of yourself. Miss you terribly. Affectionately, Trev." At least he had been okay at that time, but he must have been in the midst of heavy fighting.

I had heard from Ken the second week of January. He had been re-hospitalized because of unspecified problems with his leg. However, he expected to be discharged within days. I wrote back wishing him well. February ended with no further word from either him or Trev.

Rapidly as the reinforcements were emptying their complements of men into the war machine across the Channel and replacing them with fresh young recruits from Canada, our workload at the Selection of Personnel Office was increasing just as quickly. Our staff grew accordingly. In December we had added a couple of CWACs fresh from Canada, delighted to realize their dream of getting overseas at last. Now we added two more. It was my job to supervise the newcomers.

Although our office was busy, the atmosphere was invariably pleasant. Everyone, including our three or four male officers, was blessed with a sense of humour. No one fussed about military protocol, except when visiting brass arrived. The same was true at our barracks. Our CWAC officers took a relaxed approach. When some new requirement suddenly developed, it came from the brass at CMHQ and was never followed for long. A good example was the order for Friday afternoon's aimless marching up and down the parade ground (as mentioned earlier, this was where I disgraced myself by breaking ranks running after my hat). Some visiting VIP had decided we girls were getting sloppy and needed smartening up. After three or four weeks, those drills suddenly ended, never to be revived.

Similarly ill-fated was an order in late February 1945. We CWAC sergeants were required to take turns calling 47 Company out on parade every morning before breakfast. The evening before my turn, my date, a Signals Corps sergeant, spent two hours reviewing the procedure with me. The next morning, at 0645 hours, I stood in the middle of Grant Square and shouted, "Company, on parade!" I called the company to attention, then ordered "Right dress!" Except for the girl at the right end of each line, who kept staring straight ahead, the girls all turned their heads sharply to the right, and shuffled forwards and backwards to be perfectly in line with her.

That's all very well for male soldiers, at least young ones, whose figures go straight up and down, but women come in a variety of shapes, with all sorts of bumps and curves. A line of women never looks perfectly straight at either the front or back. My date had told me to accept any reasonable attempt when I eyed each line from the right. Then I marched the girls around and gave a few more orders, like "Forward march," "Halt," "Left turn." All went well until I tried "Right wheel,"[5] only to realize too late I hadn't allowed enough room for this manoeuvre. "Halt!" I shouted, as one end of the formation was about to march into the wall. There was only one thing to do: give up. "Company, dismiss!" I yelled. Our CWAC officers gave up, too. That was 47 Company's last morning parade.

CHAPTER FIFTEEN

IRISH SPRING

CANADIAN ARMY regulations permitted travel to Éire, a neutral country, only for those soldiers with immediate relatives there. I'm not sure why it didn't occur to Jeanne or me to lie. Goodness knows, we both told enough other lies during our military careers. Probably we just assumed lying wouldn't work. And so we devised a somewhat complicated plan. Had it gone wrong, the consequences could have been more serious than if we had lied about relatives, but we were risk-takers and, as you will already have realized, not the most sensible of young women.

Jeanne suggested that we each go to our respective orderly rooms and request passes to the most southerly town in Northern Ireland. At HQ CRU all passes were issued through the Pay Office, presided over by my friend, the genial Andy

Beck. I knew he'd once been stationed in Northern Ireland. I asked him the name of its southernmost town.

"I don't know, Doris," he said, "I was stationed way up north, never went south of Belfast. Let's check the map." He opened his desk drawer and pulled out a well-worn, crumpled booklet containing a number of small maps, including one of Ireland. We looked at the border between the North and South. The map was creased and dirty, and the letters so small we had trouble making them out. Two towns looked to be right on the border: Newry and Dundalk.

"I vote for Dundalk," said Andy. "The letters are bigger. It must be more important, more likely to be in Northern Ireland."

And so it happened that he made out my pass for "Dundalk, N. Ireland."

At about the same time, Jeanne would have been consulting a large wall map in 43 Company's orderly room, in London. Not until we were on the train heading north out of that city did we discover that our passes were for different destinations. Hers read "Newry," which was north of the border, but my "Dundalk" turned out to be not the most southerly town in Northern Ireland, after all, but rather the most northerly town in the South, in the Republic of Éire. What to do?

Ink smeared easily in those days. I dropped a spot of tea on the "N", smearing that letter nicely and then with two strokes of a pen transformed the former "N" into a shaky but passable "S". Thus, barring close inspection, I now had a valid pass to Éire. Unfortunately, Jeanne could not so easily transform her pass. Changing "Newry" to "Dundalk" would be impossible. The resulting mess would never pass scrutiny. When we got to the border, maybe she could pretend she'd lost her pass and I, with a valid one, would vouch for her. No sense in worrying about the matter now. We'd cross that bridge when we came to it.

Although there was a direct route to Éire, by ferry from Holyhead to a port near Dublin, it would be of no use to us. Because we, or at least Jeanne, would have to sneak into the forbidden country, we needed to take the long way around. Thus late one Friday evening we boarded a crowded train at Victoria Station with our bicycles, destined for some point near the Scottish border. I can't recall the name of that stop, but do remember us leaving the train early the next morning and at my insistence cycling some miles out of our way to see Robbie Burns's cottage. We needn't have bothered. The small, plain stone hut stood all by itself in the middle of a field, shut up tight, not a soul around. We rode on, heading for Stranraer and the ferry. Aided by lifts in a workman's truck and later a big army lorry, we reached the dock with less than an hour to spare.

Jeanne had insisted we book a stateroom. She had been very seasick on her Atlantic voyage and so traumatized that now, before the ferry even started moving, she took to her berth. I went out on deck. Just as when I had crossed it on the *Queen Elizabeth* two and a half years earlier, the notoriously rough Irish Sea was almost like glass. I revelled in the ship's gentle motion, the tang of the salt air, and the breeze blowing in my face and through my hair. I felt sorry for Jeanne, shut up in the stuffy cabin. However, we would both get more than our fill of fresh air in the week to follow.

The ferry took us to the little port of Larne, only about an hour's cycle from Belfast. In the city we set about locating the railway station, buying tickets to Dundalk, lunching at a small café, and picking up some cheese and crackers and a couple of sandwiches to eat en route. We had little time to spare. The last train left at three o'clock. To be in Éire as long as possible, we had to make that train.

And now we came to the second step of our plan, the bridge we had thought to cross when we came to it. How would we get Jeanne into Éire? We could both get off the train at Newry and try to sneak across the border on our bicycles, but it seemed a shame to have to resort to that, when we had tickets to Dundalk and I at least had a pass to take me there. There was only one thing to do. As soon as we approached the Newry station, Jeanne would retreat to the washroom, taking all her belongings with her. I would hold off the conductor or who-ever as long as possible, so that he might not think to check the washroom.

Accordingly we took seats at the end of the last car, very close to the exit and the washroom. Plans made, we relaxed, munched our snacks, and settled down to watch the emerald-green countryside passing by. Despite the cloudy skies, the landscape enchanted us. Then we dozed off, to wake up sud-denly as the train slowed. I glanced out the window to see a big platform sign: NEWRY! "Quick," I whispered to Jeanne, "grab your stuff and head to the washroom." Fortunately, the checking began at the front of the train, as we had hoped. It wasn't the conductor who did the checking, however, but two burly gentlemen, one an immigration officer, the other a mil-itary policeman. I took my time finding my papers, fumbling through all my pockets, and then, putting on a show of being very upset, searching frantically through my haversack before pulling them out from the spot where I knew they'd been all the time. I hoped my stalling technique would work. We hadn't considered the fact that the officials would of course know the number of passengers on the train and not rest until they had accounted for all of them.

When I finally produced my pass, the immigration officer turned it over to the military policeman and went off to bang on the washroom door. Jeanne emerged, red-faced. "Have you got the same permission?" asked the MP, as he handed my pass back to me. "Yes, I have," Jeanne lied. She looked guilty as could be, but luck was on our side. The train was behind schedule. The officers left, evidently anxious to be on their way.

Jeanne and I had just finished breathing sighs of relief when another hurdle threatened. The conductor came through the train announcing that at Dundalk we would all be required to go through customs. That wouldn't have been a problem for me, but Jeanne was carrying a professional-type camera and feared she might not be allowed to take it into the country. This was something we hadn't thought about. How were we going to evade customs? Well, surely there would be a refreshment room off the platform? Every station of any size had one. We would just slip out of the line, grab our bicycles from the luggage car, disappear into the refreshment room (taking our bicycles in with us), and lie low until the train departed and all was quiet.

Our plan worked beautifully. We sat drinking tea and relaxing comfortably for a good hour. No one had noticed our disappearance. The train had gone. All was quiet. "Well," I said to Jeanne, "I think we've sat here long enough. I'll just go out and take a look around." I sauntered down the deserted platform: not a soul anywhere in sight. Might as well take a few steps more, I said to myself. Then I saw him, at the very end of the long platform, barely visible. I could just make out the figure in blue waving its arms. Feigning nonchalance, I took a couple of steps more, then turned and headed back, only gradually increasing my pace to a fast trot. "Some guy spotted me," I told Jeanne. "I think he's headed this way." A couple of minutes later, the angry station agent burst in. "What are you girls doing here?" he demanded. "Have you been through customs?"

"Customs?" Jeanne asked in a determinedly puzzled tone, as though the word was entirely foreign to her. "You know you were supposed to go through customs," the man insisted, angrily. "Just wait here!" And off he went, leaving the door wide open. A gust of cold wind blew our paper napkins across the room.

"What's the matter with him?" asked the waitress, coming out of the kitchen. "He does it every time, leaves the door wide open." She slammed the door shut and retreated to the warmth behind the counter. We sat waiting, tense, wondering what would happen next. Suddenly there came a furious banging on the door. We couldn't make out his words, but from the force with which they were being uttered, we assumed the agent was swearing in his native language. He couldn't get the door open. We called for the waitress, but she had disappeared. Jeanne went over to try to open the door. Alas, it was locked. More swearing from the other side. Then silence. Two or three minutes later, an aproned man came in from the kitchen, politely telling us we had to leave. Behind him, the agent, face beet-red with fury, glared at us. "Come along with me," he barked.

Meekly, we followed the agent down half the length of the platform, to where stood a very large ruddy-cheeked gentleman, presumably a customs officer. He grinned broadly as we approached. "Well, now, what are you girls doing here in Ireland?" Then, in answer to our response, "Ah, Canadians, I just love Canadians. And so you've come over from England? Tell me, how are things in England these days? What about whiskey? Do they have lots of it? What's it cost?" And so we chatted on at considerable length. He was much more interested in us and our adventures and the price of whiskey than in looking through our belongings. The agent stood by, shifting from one foot to the other, scowling and gritting his teeth. Finally our genial customs man said, "Well, I guess I'm supposed to take a look at what you have here." I opened the small case strapped to the tray of my bicycle, displaying a disorderly mess of army-issue undies, pyjamas, cold cream. He glanced at it, gave it a gentle poke, nodded, and turned to bestow the same cursory attention on Jeanne's haversack. He didn't bother to look in the basket at the front of her bicycle, where the precious camera lay hidden.

"Well now, you young women have a place to stay tonight?" We shook our heads. It was beginning to get dark. "No? Well, here's what you do: follow this road about a quarter mile, where you'll see a turnoff to the left. The second house on your right belongs to Mrs. O'Hara, good friend o' mine. Tell her Liam Donnelly sent you. Sure an' she'll look after you." With that, he wished us Godspeed and a safe trip, and sent us on our way.

After a pleasant overnight stay at the B & B recommended by the jovial giant, we hopped on our trusty, rusty steeds and headed for Dublin, which we hoped to reach by nightfall. In great spirits despite the overcast sky and a few raindrops, we kept up a brisk pace for a couple of hours or more before stopping at a village bakery to pick up a few scones. Fresh milk from a nearby farm would wash them down nicely, we thought.

As with all the farms we passed, the little whitewashed cottage was set well back from the low stone wall edging the road, flanked on one side by the barn, on the other by smaller outbuildings. Thus you approached the dwelling through the muddy barnyard. The cottage door was standing ajar. Chickens wandered through at will, tracking mud over the hard-dirt kitchen floor. The cheerful farm wife poured milk into our cups, assuring us it was from that morning's milking. It was not only unpasteurized, but also stored under conditions probably less than sanitary, but this being our first fresh milk in almost two and a half years, we weren't about to question its safety. We downed it with great relish.

My atlas tells me the distance from Dundalk to Dublin is not great. Even with our very basic bicycles, we should have reached Ireland's capital in one day, but nightfall found us still many miles away. Except when having dinner at a small village pub, we hadn't made any lengthy stops. Perhaps there were too many brief pub stops, though we certainly didn't have money enough to quench our thirst often with anything but water.

At any rate, when darkness fell, we were still far from Dublin and without a place to stay. We had counted on there being some kind of lodging available in the tiny village where we had dined, but no such luck. Desperate, we tried several times to sneak into a barn, but at each attempt dogs would rush at us, barking their heads off. Finally, after the third try, we gave up and sought shelter on a hillside, inside the ruins of an old stone structure, only to plunge into a mass of stinging nettles. By this time thoroughly exhausted, we retreated to the open field, pulled our army-issue flannelette pyjamas on over our slacks and sweaters, spread raincoats on the hard, bumpy ground, and settled down to sleep. Or so we hoped.

Of course, sleep failed to come. We could have tolerated the other discomforts, but not the cold. This was March, after all, with a brisk wind blowing, to boot. When at 2:30 a.m., for the first and only time in my life, my teeth began to chatter uncontrollably, we packed the pyjamas, donned our raincoats, and got on the bikes once again. Somehow we kept going for a couple of hours along that silent, dark, deserted road, fortifying ourselves every now and then with a chocolate from a box Jeanne's folks had sent from home.

Arriving at last on the outskirts of Dublin, we stopped the first policeman we saw and asked for directions to the railway station, where we hoped at least for some warmth. Too bad, we were a good two hours early; the station didn't open until 6:30 a.m. We had to settle for a bench on a little oval concrete island at the intersection of McConnell Street and some other road whose name Jeanne and I have both forgotten. Like two abandoned waifs, we slumped disconsolately on the bench, exhausted but too cold to drop off to sleep.

"And what might ye two ladies be doin' here this time o' the night?" Standing across the street was a big burly Irish policeman, who except for his brogue might have been a London bobby, so similar was the uniform. Our accent quickly allayed his suspicions. "Ah, ye're not from this country," he said, smiling. Hearing the tale of our travels, he commented, "Well, ye're a couple of sturdy women, a couple of sturdy women is all I can say." Sympathetic to our plight, he sent us half a block down the street to a small hotel, with instructions to ring for the night porter. No luck. The night porter must have been sound asleep.

By this time shivering more than ever, I pointed to one of the two lighted telephone kiosks a few feet away and announced I was going in there to get out of the wind. Jeanne promptly established herself in the other one, where she stood reading the telephone book. I didn't have the strength for that. Instead, I squeezed myself into a hunched-up sitting position on the floor and fell sound asleep immediately, dead to the world until Jeanne hammered on the door and woke me at a quarter after six. She told me she had just reached the bottom of page 1 of the telephone book when a roughly dressed fellow banged on her door, informing her, "The girl in the next one has conked out!"

"No," she told him, "she's just sleeping!"

On to the railway station we pedalled, slightly refreshed after our rest but still chilly. What a relief to find in the ladies' lounge two leather sofas set against the walls, at right angles to each other. Jeanne flopped down on one, I on the other, nearest the door. Finding the light quite bright and thinking I'd sleep better with my head covered, I pulled a discarded newspaper over it and promptly fell into a deep sleep.

I awoke with a start to feel someone yanking roughly on my left leg, as the newspaper slid off my head. A male voice gasped, "Oh, it's a girl!" As was the case with many public lavatories at the time, Dublin's railway station employed a full-time attendant for the women's. When this lady arrived for work, she had taken one look and run to find a male employee to oust "two tramps" from the women's lounge.

Since we were in this neutral country illegally, Jeanne and I had tried to dress inconspicuously. You would think our experience in the railway station would have given us a clue, but not until a couple of days later, when followed down a street by a horde of noisy kids and dogs, did we realize we were sticking out like sore thumbs, or at least I was. At first we couldn't make out what the kids were yelling, but their gestures told us it had something to do with my clothing. Were they saying something about "slacks"? We weren't sure until later, when a delightful couple who took us into their home explained that Irish women never, ever wore slacks unless out in the country somewhere, working in the fields. Jeanne, in her jodhpurs, was more acceptably attired.

After our night's accommodation in the field, telephone kiosks, and railway station, we were feeling, and doubtless looking, decidedly grubby and much in need of a hot bath. Having been informed by the kindly woman attendant that only two hotels in the entire city had hot water, we headed for the Victoria, closest of the two, only to be turned away. The hotel was full, the clerk said. Suspecting a lie and not wanting to miss out on our one remaining chance of a hot bath, Jeanne telephoned the other hotel and in her most dignified tone asked to reserve a double room. This ploy worked. Having earlier promised a room, the hotel staff there could hardly turn us away, however appalled they might have been by our grubby appearance. The Shelbourne was half empty, as were probably

The Shelbourne Hotel was one of only two Dublin
hotels able to provide hot water for baths.

all the hotels in the city—with or without hot water.

Never have I enjoyed a bath so much. I must have soaked for an hour. The baths, followed by an hour or two of sleep plus a substantial lunch, restored our spirits and off we went on a tour of the city. I recall little of that self-guided tour, but one experience stands out. Jeanne, an avid photographer even in those days, thrilled to the sight in this neutral country of the German Embassy, with its armed guard in Nazi uniform marching up and down in front. What a great shot this will be, she thought. She aimed her camera at the guard. The guard in turn aimed his gun at her. Jeanne took off with all possible speed, me at her heels!

Sometime during the afternoon, wandering along a street by the canal, we spotted a BED AND BREAKFAST sign, offering accommodation at a very reasonable price. Although a far cry from the Shelbourne, the place appeared respectable enough and was much more within our price range. Happy with the second-floor room and its view of the canal and picturesque array of small fishing boats, we deposited our luggage, such as it was, on the double bed. We planned later to toss a coin as to who got that bed and who took the cot set against the adjoining wall.

Dinner at a nearby restaurant proved superb: lamb chops, plenty of potatoes, and gravy and greens, followed by real ice cream and tasty little cakes. What luxury! In a happy mood, we walked around for a while, stopping in at Rooney's where we admired the Connemara marble but could afford nothing. When we returned to our room, we discovered, to our horror, that in Ireland "bed and breakfast" evidently meant just that, not "room and breakfast"! By the cot stood a pair of large, sturdy-looking shoes. They looked suspiciously like a man's. Surely the proprietor wouldn't put a man in our room?

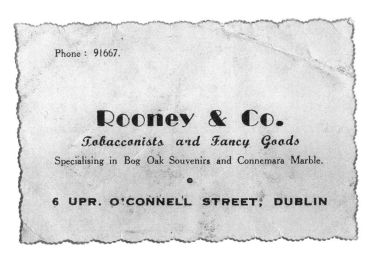

We couldn't afford to buy "bog oak" or "marble," but
the young lady behind the counter was fascinated by
our accents and treated us like valued customers.

By this time, fatigue was taking hold again. It was ten o'clock at night. We didn't have the energy to go searching for other accommodation, if indeed we could have found any at that hour. Jeanne put on her pyjamas at great speed and leapt into the double bed, grabbing the side closest to the wall. I hopped in immediately after. The two of us lay there wide awake for a good half-hour before we heard someone creep in and settle onto the cot without turning on the light. There followed a strange metallic clicking sound that went on for several minutes and puzzled us both.

In the morning we met our roommate. She was a pleasant little middle-aged woman from the country, dressed all in black as many seemed to be. We never did quite figure out the shoes, but speculated that maybe they were her husband's, brought in for repair. The mysterious metallic sound? That was easily explained by the rosary on the bedside table.

CHAPTER SIXTEEN

EXITING ÉIRE

STUDYING THE MAP over breakfast that morning, we decided to explore as much of the countryside south of Dublin as could be covered in a day. Accordingly we took a train to Greystones, seventeen miles south of Dublin, our starting point for a delightful cycle through Rocky Valley and the Sugar Loaf and other mountains (hills, really) of lovely Wicklow County. We would like to have stopped and climbed one of those hills on foot, but time did not permit. Jeanne settled for a picture instead. Some thirty years later she was to present me with an oil painting she had done from that picture. It remains one of my most treasured souvenirs.

We would have loved to cycle farther south, but our time was limited and so in the early afternoon we turned back toward Dublin. A tip from a peripatetic Englishman we met along the way took us through the equally pretty district around Enniskerry. A light rain soon gave way to high cloud and intermittent sunshine, enough to brighten the rolling landscape without generating too much warmth, ideal for cycling through hilly country.

I don't recall all the details of that day, but the evening stands out in memory. As usual, we had no special itinerary and no place to stay. We should perhaps have learned from our previous experience, when we had to sleep, or try to, in a field, but being young and foolhardy we counted on finding accommodation in the small village we reached around seven in the evening. Again, there was none to be had. Desperate, we told our sad story to a policeman on the street. "What about the local lock-up?" I ventured to ask. "Would you have room there?" He responded in the negative, with a chuckle, and then said, "I tell you what, you girls just come home with me. My wife's English and she would love to hear what's happening in England these days."

And so, we walked our bicycles down a couple of side streets with the kindly policeman to his comfortable home and jolly, hospitable wife. Not only did we enjoy excellent sleeping accommodation, but also a wonderful dinner and pleasant evening chatting by the fire. They both, the wife especially, had many questions for us about Canada as well as England. At one point, she turned to him, and enthused, "Pat, aren't these girls wonderful, coming all this way to fight for us?" He roared back in protest, "They're not fighting for us! This is a neutral country!" But it was said with a laugh, and a wink for us. The war in Europe was almost over at this point, and everyone knew how it would end. I suspect most of the Irish had hoped for a long time that it would end as it did.

The next day this hospitable couple fed us a traditional Irish breakfast with all the trimmings, and sent us on our way with a box lunch and hearty good wishes. I can't remember if we wrote to them later. We certainly should have. I hope we did, and I hope they continued to live happy, healthy lives in their pretty village.

By this time we were becoming concerned about getting back to barracks on time. Only three days to make it all the way back to London! As we dared not try re-crossing the border by train, we felt compelled to cycle across it and thence to Belfast. Thus we pedalled our fastest from Enniskerry to Dublin, where we would take the train as far as Drogheda. We reached Dublin with forty-five minutes to spare, giving us time to look around the railway station.

There, we observed a display that had escaped our notice on the previous visit. Extending the entire length of one wall, near the top, a row of identical posters beamed an unmistakable message down at us. Each bore an outline map of Ireland, the large bottom portion painted a solid emerald green, the tiny portion at the top depicting Ulster covered by the red, white, and blue Union Jack. Beneath, the caption in large black capital letters read OUT OF PLACE! However, except for the hostile station agent in Dundalk and the children who had followed us shouting criticism of my attire, the Irish people we encountered in the Republic never once made us feel out of place. On the contrary, they gave us the warmest of welcomes.

From Dublin we travelled by train to Drogheda, and then by bicycle to Dunlear, where we stayed in a room above a store. It was comfortable enough, though lacking electricity.

I had a special reason for wanting to stop in Drogheda. On our way down I'd bought a beautiful green suede jacket there. Unfortunately, after a couple of hours of cycling I had been horrified to discover huge rents under the arms. I now hoped for at least a partial refund. We arrived at the store at ten to six, ten minutes before closing time, asking to see the manager. He was adamant. I must have abused the garment. Their stock was always of the highest quality. "No," I insisted, "I do not abuse clothing. This garment is defective." The two of us stood there facing each other, neither with the slightest intention of giving in. Six o'clock came and went. He kept repeating that the fault was mine. I kept repeating that the garment was defective. Ten after six, a quarter after six, and still we continued. Finally, no doubt suffering pangs of hunger and picturing the juicy steak awaiting him at home, this obdurate man facing an equally obdurate dissatisfied customer, offered a fifteen per cent discount. Racked with hunger pangs myself by this time, I readily accepted. Later, back in Canada, someone mended that jacket. Although it didn't bear close scrutiny, it nevertheless gave me several years of wear.

∾

In the Shamrock Isle, to know what side of the border you're on, just look for the post boxes. In Ulster they are red, in Éire green. At least, that's the way it was then. On our return trip, Jeanne and I crossed from South to North not once, but twice. Unintentionally the second time, of course. Arriving around ten in the morning at a town we took to be Newry, we had stopped in the middle of a bridge to ask a pedestrian the location of the customs and immigration office for Éire. "Oh, over there," he said, "just go right by like everyone else!" More than once Jeanne and I had noted this Irish delight in aiding and abetting lawbreakers, at least when it came to minor infractions. We cycled on by, but then, expecting the customs office for Ulster to be along this same route, veered off onto side roads, presumably more or less parallel to the main one. At any rate, we seemed to be heading north, and the red post boxes told us we had arrived safely in Ulster.

On and on we went, puffing up steep hills and coasting down long slopes in the Mountains of Mourne. The scenery was gorgeous. Jeanne took several pictures. I still have one of them. But time was getting on and the winding roads made it difficult to determine exactly where we were. That main road we had originally been travelling alongside was nowhere to be found. Suddenly I stopped. "Jeanne," I said, "what do you see on that corner and what colour is it?"

"What do you mean? It's a green mailbox, so what?"

"Jeanne, what colour are the mailboxes in Northern Ireland?"

"Oh!" Jeanne slumped on her bicycle. "Oh, no!"

In desperately trying to evade customs, we had circled around and landed back in Éire. Somehow we found our way back to the road on which we had originally approached Newry, and to the same bridge where we had made our earlier queries. We had gone full circle. Again we found an obliging pedestrian. We told him we knew where the customs office for Éire was, but where was the one for Ulster? "In the same building," he said, "at the north end. Just go on past it." We'd wasted four or five hours and an immense amount of energy trying to avoid a customs office we'd already passed!

By this time quite exhausted, we had to rest a while before dinner. We ate at half past five, an absurdly early hour for Irish restaurants in those days, but we were starving and luckily found a pub willing to feed us whenever. Even though now in Ulster, we still had steak and also milk, presumably from local farms. Full stomachs having restored our spirits, we set out once more, just as it was growing dark. Belfast, here we come! Unlike the night we cycled into Dublin when the moon had occasionally appeared briefly between clouds, there was no moon and we rode along in the pitch black, not a light to be seen anywhere. We had been going about an hour when a cyclist heading south warned, "Watch out, there's a patrol up ahead!"

Jeanne and I stopped and held a hurried, whispered conference. Here once more we faced a hurdle we hadn't anticipated. What questions would they ask us? Would they interrogate us together or separately? What would they do if they discovered we'd been in Éire? Our lies had to agree. Was the patrol stationary? Maybe it was coming toward us? Hoping we hadn't been overheard, we moved on.

For a few minutes we pedalled in silence, not daring to speak. Suddenly, a gruff male voice rang out: "Halt!" Blinded by the painfully bright light of at least half a dozen torches, as the British called them, we jammed on our brakes.

"Who are you and what are you doing here?" a voice demanded. The questioners could see us, but we couldn't see them. A second voice fired another question: "Where are your bicycle lights?" We were ready for that one. "Someone in Newry stole them." That was a lie, of course. We had never had lights. With no traffic on the roads, we didn't need any. Our

timid replies and Canadian accent may have made things easier for us, but it was a good ten or fifteen minutes before they
let us continue on our way. That was only the first of many such
delays. By the time we staggered into Belfast, we had encountered twenty-one patrols, each equally demanding. After half a
dozen lying recitations, we began to save time by anticipating
the questions and coming out with a canned speech, sounding
like parrots or newly minted salesmen. I chuckled inwardly
at Jeanne's rapid, tired monotone: "My name is Jeanne White.
I'm on leave from the Canadian Women's Army Corps and
I'm going to Belfast on my way back to barracks in London.
We spent our leave cycling in the mountains north of Newry.
Someone stole our bicycle lights last night."

It was 1:30 a.m. when we pedalled into Belfast, as usual
with no place to stay. We stopped a Canadian naval officer walking along the street, to ask for advice. Following his
detailed directions, we easily found the Grand Central Hotel.
While I was stacking our bicycles up against the wall, Jeanne
did as the officer had suggested, threading her way through
the motley group milling around the entrance to press the bell
for the night porter. When the door opened, she asked, "May
we have a room together please?" Why she put it just like that
I will never know, but of course, like me, she was thoroughly
exhausted. The phrasing proved unfortunate. In her tired state
she'd thought I was the person standing beside her, whereas in
reality it was a dignified middle-aged gentleman who had just
emerged from a cab, cigar in hand. "No!" exclaimed the porter, slamming the door shut. Jeanne turned to me, eyes blazing,
"What are you doing over there? Come here!" and rang for the
porter once more. "I mean this girl and me," she stammered,

Receipt from the Grand Central Hotel where
Jeanne nearly acquired a male roomate.

red-faced. In we went. I have often wondered what that well-dressed gentleman thought of Jeanne's original request.

The rest was anti-climax. A short ride to the port of Larne, ferry across the Irish Sea, train to London, and finally arrival at our respective barracks, that's all pretty much of a blur for us both. I do have a picture of the train's interior, another of Jeanne's snapshots. It was not divided into compartments as were most English trains at that time, but open, with passengers seated in groups of four, facing each other across a table. In the snapshot, many of them, almost all in uniform of one service or another, appear to be sleeping, heads cradled in their arms, down on the tables. No doubt we followed suit.

I've experienced many interesting trips since then, but none to compare with that Irish adventure over sixty-five years ago. We were young, eager adventurers, ready for whatever came our way. The lack of planning added to the fun. We never knew what might happen next. Thank you, Jeanne. It was your idea in the first place!

In contrast to us, Nano, the Canadian Air Force veteran I met years later, exaggerated the strength of her Irish roots, obtained a legitimate pass to Éire and travelled the short, easy route by ferry direct from England to a port near Dublin. She enjoyed her leave, but I'm sure she had nowhere near as much fun!

CHAPTER SEVENTEEN

THE GOLDEN SUMMER

FITTINGLY, VE DAY DAWNED sparkling clear and sunny. Except for cooks and other essential personnel, we all had the day off to celebrate. We climbed aboard jeeps and trucks and drove around the area, singing and waving to people on the streets, thronged into pubs, or—in the case of many sergeants and other NCOs above the rank of corporal—crowded into the sergeants' mess. Some stayed the whole day in that little recreational centre, consuming amazing quantities of beer, though I don't recall more than two or three celebrants becoming truly sozzled.

Shortly before VE Day (Victory in Europe), we had begun to see on the village streets a number of wan, emaciated young men, liberated from German prisoner of war camps. Many more were to arrive in the ensuing weeks. Those in condition to do so were free to come and go as they pleased from neighbouring Basingstoke military hospital, where they were housed. Most looked ashen and painfully thin. I watched one fellow, fiancé of a CWAC friend, raise his arm for a salute. I could have sworn I saw the light through his hand. The majority were apathetic and listless, mentally as well as physically exhausted. They had little energy even for conversation.

There were exceptions, however. I vividly recall one man, who didn't look in the least undernourished, rampaging through the area, shouting what a rotten country England was and why didn't they let him go back to Germany? This behaviour continued on and off for a number of days. His wording never changed. No one paid much attention; we all realized he must have become unhinged by whatever experiences he had come through.[1]

It was only after VE Day that we CWACs began to think seriously of what the future might hold. Up until then, one day had followed same as the other, and it seemed as if we might go on this way forever. Now, suddenly, this way of life was coming to an end. War in the East was still raging. Some in our company began talking about volunteering for the Pacific arena. I was not among them. I detested hot weather.

Some of my colleagues had become so fond of England and the English that they wanted to stay. They talked of running a pub in some quaint little village. That was all wishful thinking, but something I understood. I wasn't eager to leave this land either. Still, I had to face the inevitability of returning to Canada and to civilian life, with all its uncertainties. Consequently, when news of educational and other post-discharge benefits came filtering down to us from headquarters,

I immediately put in a request for early return and discharge. With luck, I might be able to resume my studies at UBC in September, room and board paid for by VA (Veterans Affairs) grants. I would have my BA by the following spring. I wrote letters to the appropriate authorities, but at this point no one could give me an answer.

Nevertheless, I had qualms. How well would I readjust to civilian life? Would I be able to retain the level of self-confidence military experience had given me? What kind of social life would I have back in Vancouver? All my old pals were now either married or engaged. One was expecting her first baby. My only single friends with no marital plans were my army buddies, from whom I would soon be separated. My parents had moved to a different neighbourhood. I certainly was not planning to live at home, but their present residence would be yet another change in the landscape.

I did regret having come this far and failing to make it across the Channel. Perhaps it was this feeling that impelled Jeanne and our friend Myrtle to spend our next—and as it turned out, final—overseas leave on the south coast in the Ramsgate-Dover area, the closest we could get to France. We stayed at a small seafront hotel in Ramsgate. Now, with these eastern beaches finally freed of their barbed-wire barriers, we could go for another dip in the sea, like the one the three of us had enjoyed at Bournemouth the previous August.[2]

The white cliffs of Dover were but a short cycle away. We couldn't leave England without seeing them. From Dover beach we gazed longingly across at the barely visible coast of Normandy. If only we had been able to get over there!

Shortly after returning from this March leave, I had found

myself in a lengthy after-dinner conversation with Reggie, a fellow from the regimental accounts office. We sat talking in the sergeants' mess for an hour or more, mostly about his experiences in Italy the previous year. He had been one of the "D-Day Dodgers,"[3] as they called themselves.

As I learned later, however, Reggie had never experienced combat. He'd remained well behind the lines. Older than most of the front-line soldiers and a competent bookkeeper, he held a desk job as keeper of regimental accounts, still his role at HQ CRU. In the fall of 1944, he'd been sent back to England for officers' training. It was a huge disappointment to him when he failed the course. He said it was because he'd flunked the obstacle test. I suspected he had spent too long behind a desk, missing much of the routine drilling and training of the average soldier. Perhaps he had also drunk too much *vino* and dallied excessively with the Italian damsels.

As he walked me to my barracks, my new acquaintance confided that his English fiancée was about to get a divorce from her long-absent husband, serving with the British Army abroad. She had applied over three years earlier, not long after meeting this Canadian soldier, but British law required the elapse of that amount of time before the divorce could be final. I found Reggie a pleasant conversationalist. However, he was balding, looked at least thirty and thus too old for me, and was involved with someone else. I thought no more about him.

A couple of weeks before my June leave, Reggie sought me out to announce that he was now "a free man." He and his fiancée had broken up. According to him they had been having more and more conflicts, and finally she said she could no longer tolerate his constant fault-finding. He didn't elaborate further, except to say that she was given to moodiness, often saying extremely hurtful things. He said they were incompatible, a fact he should have realized earlier. He asked me for a date. I put him off tactfully.

On the romantic front, my situation was far from exciting. I was also still trying to find out what had happened to Trev. A returned prisoner of war told me one group in his POW camp had come from Trev's unit. Several, badly wounded, had been moved to a POW hospital. He didn't know their names. From my description, he thought one might have been Trev, but couldn't be sure. He also said that prior to the men's capture, four of their tanks had been blown up. I wanted to hope, but feared the worst. As for Ken, I had heard nothing since early March. Although unable to completely forget or forgive his odd behaviour at the hospital, I still valued his friendship. I worried about him. It wasn't like him to go so long without writing.

Reggie was persistent. A few months earlier, when I'd had so many interesting fellows to choose from, he wouldn't have stood a chance. However, at this point there was no one on the scene except George, a twenty-four-year-old rendered unfit for battle because of a vision problem. George had nothing but good looks to recommend him, and I was in the process of writing him off anyway, because I had caught him in the process of two-timing me with a CWAC private in 47 Company. Unaware that I knew, he may have wondered why I refused his next request for a date. I was happy to let him wonder. Thus Reggie had no competition. And so, a few days before my leave when he asked again, I accepted, although reluctantly. Never had I dated anyone so old or with so little hair!

Reggie turned out to be surprisingly interesting. Although never in combat, he did experience a frightening enemy attack en route to Italy, when his troopship was hit by an aerial torpedo and a bomb simultaneously. I still have his typewritten account of that trip. I reprint some lightly edited excerpts here, not only for their inherent interest, but also for the light they throw on his personality:

> A terrific crash shook the ship. The huge vessel lurched upward and forward as though it wanted to leap right out of the water. Most of the lights went out...sound of crashing glass everywhere.... The ship heaved violently to port... unmistakable smell of cordite.... Being trapped in the bowels of a sinking ship gives even the bravest man a feeling of helplessness.... Found our way to a crowded staircase...reached an open deck...personnel started leaving the ship, but it seemed a slow, orderly operation, so back to the cabin for a salvage operation.... I put on my civilian shoes,[4] got my flashlight, wallet and camera...back on deck...went down the scramble net only to reach the waterline as a lifeboat from a destroyer pulled away full, so I had to swim out twenty or thirty feet and bring a raft that had been cut loose earlier back to the scramble net. The raft quickly filled up with a dozen lads and off we shoved with only one paddle between us...not the kind of raft that keeps you dry, only keeps you from sinking, but at this time the Mediterranean waters were warm enough to be tolerable.

Reggie describes how they drifted aimlessly for three hours before coming across a large box raft that would keep them out of the water. It was now dark. Even with this raft's three paddles they could make little headway, and were becoming colder and increasingly uncomfortable when finally a lifeboat from a rescue ship picked them up:

Tired out, cold and wet, I faced a scramble net slung over the side of the Empire State Building. No fooling, it appeared that high! Gritting my teeth, I grabbed at the net at the wrong moment and found myself in the sea. Then I grabbed again and began scrambling up. On and on I went, not daring to look up or down. Finally I reached the top, completely played out. If there had been another yard I might not have made it.

A huge welcoming committee supplied us each with a towel, dry clothes, hot coffee, and most important a bunk. I was soon sound asleep. It was later reported that a torpedo from a U-boat had skipped across the bow of our ship while she was waiting to pick up the last of the survivors.

The boys were swapping stories of their adventures. Some tales were clearly the product of over-imaginative minds, but a few humorous ones were later confirmed: the little Captain, who hadn't known how to swim until this incident, doing a homemade dog paddle to a crowded raft fifty feet from the sinking ship, where he was literally kicked away and told by a private to find himself another raft, which he meekly did; the dental officer, a Colonel, who had one of his teeth kicked out by the heavy army boots of the fellow following him down the scramble net; the suave Major who escaped without getting his feet wet and even managed to salvage two bottles of scotch whiskey.

When we finally docked in Italy, our little gang danced lightly down the gangplank, not a pound of equipment to burden us. But the feeling of relief at stepping on terra firma once again was a sensation long to be remembered.

This story and Reggie's vivid word-pictures of Naples, Vesuvius, and Pompeii, the hilltop villages he and his fellow soldiers passed en route to Naples, the peasants, shopkeepers, and their families, and everyday life in Italy fascinated me. Accustomed as I had become in recent weeks to uninspiring conversationalists, I found his narrative skill refreshing, as if I had happened suddenly upon an oasis in a desiccated land. He also had a way of gazing at you intently, steadily, looking you straight in the eye. I found this interesting, but did not allow it to impress me unduly. I knew it could be deceptive.[5]

After my return from leave, Reggie became my steady date. Both members of the sergeants' mess, we saw each other not only in the evenings, but also at breakfast, lunch, and supper —in fact, almost every waking moment when not in our offices or on some kind of military errand. I had not forgotten Trev. How could I ever forget him? And what had happened to Ken? I never mentioned any of these fellows to Reggie. My experience with Ken at the hospital had taught me the wisdom of keeping some things to myself.

We spent our evenings together, often cycling in the surrounding area, punting on the canal, walking "the military mile" into Aldershot to attend a movie or drop into one of the pubs, or sometimes just chatting in the sergeants' mess. On a couple of weekends we travelled by train and bike to picnic spots along the Thames. I shall always associate the signing of the Magna Carta with beer-soaked sandwiches, since it was at Runnymede that I clumsily tipped Reggie's open and almost full bottle over on our picnic lunch. He just laughed it off and dismissed my abject apologies. A good-natured chap, I thought.

Inevitably, with such close and constant association, the relationship intensified rapidly. In a mere two or three weeks, Reggie began talking about his expectations on arriving home and how soon we might be married. He declared himself entirely in favour of my academic aspirations. Perhaps I could have my UBC credits transferred to Toronto, where he had a job awaiting him with the insurance company where he had worked prior to enlistment. His company, like many others, promised returning veterans their old jobs back after discharge. If I needed to stay at UBC for the one year needed to obtain my degree, that was still okay with him. We could be married in the spring.

Reggie was even more nervous than I about returning to civilian life. He had been overseas the best part of six years. His home situation had changed drastically. His mother had died the previous year when he was in Italy, and his father had remarried only six months later, greatly distressing Reggie and his sister as well as all the family friends. Already engaged at the time Reggie enlisted in the fall of 1939, his sister was now married and the mother of two small children. All but one of his old friends were married, most of them now also parents. Reggie said, plaintively, "Aside from my job, I have nothing to go back to." In retrospect, it seems obvious that we were both looking for something, or someone, to hang onto. But it wasn't obvious to me then. I was too deeply involved emotionally to be that objective.

We discussed our dreams, our aspirations, our values, in great detail. We agreed on having children once I had my degree and he'd had a year to settle back into civilian life. We agreed on the kind of home we'd like to have, the way we'd manage our finances, everything I could think of that one should discuss in advance of marriage. Reggie spoke of his happy childhood, with an adored and adoring sister, as well as loving parents and grandparents. I looked forward to a warm welcome from this fine family, whose only problem seemed to be the father's recent remarriage. No doubt time would ease that difficulty.

I had learned to overlook Reggie's thinning hair. Once you did that, he was quite good-looking. I was madly in love and anticipated a happy life ahead. "Madly" is exactly the right word. My letters home that summer are an embarrassment to read. I can only plead insanity.

We made two or three weekend trips to London, where we visited Reggie's aunt in her little apartment. He introduced me with the words: "I want you to meet the newest member of the family." That same weekend we went shopping for an engagement ring. The prices, for even a tiny diamond, shocked us. Knowing Reggie's limited funds, I suggested it would be smarter to wait until I arrived home, since my dad did accounts for a Vancouver jeweller who would doubtless give us a discount. I didn't mind waiting.

Our final visit to London coincided with a momentous occasion. While walking along Oxford Street towards Marble Arch, we suddenly became engulfed by crowds of people pouring out of the Underground, descending from buses, thronging onto roads and sidewalks from all directions. Above us, people squeezed together in open windows, shouting and singing and waving flags and streamers. It was VJ Day (Victory over Japan). The war in the Pacific was over.

Earlier that day, Reggie had asked me to carry his camera in my purse. I had been reluctant, protesting lack of room. Our tiny army-issue purses barely accommodated wallet and lipstick, but somehow he squeezed the camera in, a deed he was later to regret. After lunch at the Marble Arch Lyons' Corner House, I went downstairs to the washroom, jam-packed like every other place that day. To get at my compact and lipstick, I had to take out the camera. Appallingly, I forgot to put it back in. I remembered by the time I reached the top of the stairs and ran back, but by then it was too late. The camera was gone. In those days, it was irreplaceable. How sad, I think today. That camera had survived both the Blitz and the Italian campaign, only to be lost by me in London on VJ Day.

I was almost in tears, telling this sad story to my beau. Although at first understandably crestfallen, he very quickly recovered his usual calm demeanour and concentrated on trying to make me feel better. It wasn't the end of the world, he said. I wasn't to give it another thought. He wanted me, us, to go ahead and enjoy the day. I appreciated his considerate attitude. He seemed more concerned about my feelings than his loss.

Later that day, we happened quite by accident on a very special procession. For the second time in the course of my stay in England, I thrilled at the sight of the Royal Family. This time they rode along streets lined with spectators, travelling with much pomp and ceremony in a gilded horse-drawn carriage, preceded by cavalry in full dress uniform. They were riding to the opening of the British Parliament, an event that just happened to coincide with the VJ Day celebrations.

I found this experience less exciting than that other occasion, two years earlier, when we four girls standing alone on the curb outside our barracks had had the Royal Family all to ourselves, their smiles and waves only for us. Nevertheless, I delighted at the sight of the current procession. Reggie was less enthralled. He thought Elizabeth looked sullen and bad-tempered, in contrast to the smiling Margaret Rose. I suspected that Elizabeth as heir to the throne was already feeling the weight of future responsibility.

∾

A week or two earlier, I had finally received a letter from Ken. Written by a nurse, it told of his having been seriously wounded, back in April, shortly before VE Day. Only now had he recovered sufficiently to dictate a letter. In it, he talked of how over the past three years we'd always been there for each other and how very much that had meant to him. Although still extremely ill and facing months of hospitalization, he expected to pull through. He'd promised himself on enlistment to make no commitments to anyone until the war was over, but he hoped when we returned home we could get together "for a good, long, heart-to-heart talk." He ended by saying he expected to be on a hospital ship heading for Canada within a week or two.

While hardly a love letter, it suggested I might mean more to Ken than I'd realized. Or perhaps the sentiments expressed merely reflected a badly wounded soldier's need to find comfort. I put off writing. What could I say to this man, still so ill? All the time I'd been in England, I had thought of him only as a good friend. Until that hospital incident, he'd never given me the slightest reason to suspect he might feel anything more. We had been great comrades. We had shared a lot. But then, had we really? We'd shared anecdotes. I told him about "The Amorous Pole" and he told me about the "wonderful girl" who turned out to be a high-class prostitute. We'd had a lot of laughs. But I had never told him about Trev. And he had never mentioned anyone who was more than a passing fancy. Maybe we didn't know each other as well as I assumed we did.

Although our Selection of Personnel Office clerical staff of six had now been cut to three, our workload had also been lightened considerably. Consequently, Aileen, Connie, and I had time on our hands. I could now catch up on my correspondence without cutting into my time with Reggie. First, I had to write to Ken. A couple of weeks had gone by since his letter had arrived. It was hard to know what to say, but thinking of all he had already suffered, and what still lay ahead of him, I wrote what I hoped was a caring and thoughtful letter. I soft-pedalled my attachment to Reggie, simply saying an "interesting fellow" had asked me to marry him, but nothing was going to happen at this stage. I promised to see Ken as soon as I could after arriving home, wished him well, and added that I'd be looking forward to our "heart-to-heart talk."

In those days, however, my mind was focused on Reggie. My staff sergeant boss, Gen, had not liked him. Before she left, she told me how concerned she was for me. "Look at Reggie's face in repose," she said. "You can tell he's bad-tempered just by looking at him. I wouldn't trust him for one minute. How do you know you'll ever see him again, once you're back in Canada?" I didn't listen. I resented her remarks. I could see no basis for them. My head was in the clouds. Reggie was one of the most intriguing men I had met. He had been very calm and understanding on a couple of occasions when he might have been justified in expressing anger. He had wanted to buy me a ring. Gen, five years older than I, was a very religious, straitlaced person, a teetotaller who strongly disapproved of the drinking that went on in the sergeants' mess. She was engaged to an equally straitlaced fellow. I told myself she just couldn't accept a fun-loving character like Reggie.

I asked myself what it was about Reggie that I found so irresistible. Suppose Trev were to reappear, and just suppose he were free. How would I react? He and Reggie were not in the least alike. Trev was quieter, more serious, more contemplative. He would offer suggestions as to how we would spend our time, but usually seek out my ideas first. He made me feel cherished, in a way no one had ever done before. We had a lot in common. We both loved theatre, music, poetry, the arts in general. But all that was irrelevant now. I had to stop thinking about Trev, who had never truly been mine. Reggie was here. I was sure he loved me. Why would he have introduced me to his aunt as "the newest member of the family" if he weren't serious? Why had he wanted to buy me a ring? If he were as bad-tempered as Gen believed, how had he managed to remain so calm when I lost his precious camera?

Nevertheless, one morning when I arrived early for breakfast and only my friend Andy Beck, the pay sergeant, was in the mess, I asked him what he thought of Reggie. "Well, Doris, I hardly know him. He's never interacted much with the rest of us, spends most of his time reading the paper.[6] I only know there's no love lost between him and the officer he works for." Later, when the opportunity arose, I asked Reggie about that officer. "Can't stand him," Reggie said, flatly.

"What's the problem?" I asked.

"Oh, he's always trying to get me to line up women for him." That seemed strange. I had only seen the officer from a distance, but he looked presentable enough and younger than Reggie. He certainly had more hair! Why would he be calling on his sergeant to seek out dates for him? It seemed contrary to protocol. An officer did not put himself in a position where he would be beholden to someone under his command, particularly anyone below officer status. However, what did all that matter? I dropped the subject.

During the final week of August, Reggie and I were transferred, each to a different camp, preparatory to return to Canada and discharge. We both left England on the fourth of September, but on different ships, arriving in Halifax at different times, and leaving it on trains bound for different destinations. In the absence of compelling reasons for doing otherwise, the armed forces transported returning military personnel to the original point of enlistment. Thus I returned to Vancouver, Reggie to Toronto.

CHAPTER EIGHTEEN

GOING HOME

THE OCEAN VOYAGE contrasted sharply with that of December 1942. Not only was the sea smooth all the way and the weather sunny and warm, but the whole atmosphere had changed. The unhurried *Nieuw Amsterdam* waiters presented us with menus, which, although offering little choice, listed foods more varied and appetizing than on the trip over. Sleeping accommodation differed little, but during the day, instead of being roped off in a corner of the officers' lounge, we girls were free to mingle as we wished. At this point, nobody worried about us contaminating the officer ranks. We even ate in the officers' dining room. We spent pleasant hours in the lounge and on deck chatting with the elite—almost entirely male and mostly Air Force, as I recall. That is, we chatted with those not thoroughly immersed in a novel that most were reading, entitled *Fanny Hill*. A new edition of that eighteenth-century classic must have just come out in England. At that time it was banned in the U.S. and Canada.

No longer considered a menace to officers of whichever sex,
on the voyage home we were permitted to mingle freely.

From the now famous Pier 21 in Halifax, we marched straight to the waiting train, its engine and cars immense after the little English trains to which we had grown accustomed. On we scrambled into the car that would be our home for the next seven days. During that week the train would grow shorter and shorter, as returning Forces personnel left us at or near their hometowns. Now and again, there would be only a whistle stop, with two or three or four people waiting beside a car on a dusty road.

Some towns greeted us with music, often a pipe band. At almost every stop, kindly women would come on board with trays of home-baked scones and muffins and tarts, and all kinds of other goodies like chewing gum and chocolate bars. Our taste buds hadn't feasted on such an array of delights in years—two or three for most of us girls, five or more for some of the guys.

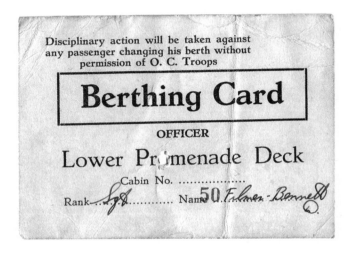

My "Berthing Card," now as a sergeant, on the
Nieuw Amsterdam on my return to Canada.

What impressed me more than the food, however, were the dramas enacted at every stop, where men and women left the train to be greeted by family and friends. One scene in particular stands out: I watched a young corporal struggling along the platform, knapsack on his back, dragging one duffle bag and carrying the other on his shoulder. Suddenly he tossed one bag to his right, the other to his left, and ran full speed into the arms of a beautiful young woman. Fiancée, wife perhaps? Tears came to my eyes. I hope the joy of that moment remained with them throughout their lives.

My mood on this journey was entirely different from my mood on the trip in the opposite direction in 1942. Then the overruling emotion, for all of us CWACs, was one of elation and tremendous excitement. Now I could not ignore the fear lurking at the back of my mind. Fear of what? I was looking forward to renewing my studies, getting my degree, at which time I would also be getting that other title, "Mrs." I had complete confidence in Reggie and the success of these plans. But for the first time in three and a half years, I didn't know who I was. I was already mourning the loss of my army identity. I wanted to slow down the train, to delay the unwelcome though inevitable transition to the anonymity of civilian life. I tried hard to push these thoughts and feelings to the far recesses of my mind.

As we rolled on across the vast land that is Canada, I marvelled at its immensity. Travelling by train is the best way to fully appreciate this land of ours. Years later I would fly from Newfoundland to Vancouver, with only a two-hour stopover in Toronto, in clear weather that permitted an almost uninterrupted view of the country spread out like a map below me. Awe-inspiring though that was, nothing could quite match the thrill of experiencing Canada by train after almost three years on the other side of the Atlantic.

One morning we awoke to the majesty and lushness of British Columbia. We had missed viewing the Rockies, but were too happy to be in our home province to give them a second thought. Thanks to a friendly conductor, another CWAC and I enjoyed much of B.C.'s glorious scenery from the cab of the caboose, humble predecessor of the dome car.

The few of us left at journey's end dragged our belongings up the long flight of stairs into the pillared concourse of Vancouver's Canadian Pacific Railway terminal. Only a small group greeted us, but what those people lacked in numbers they made up for in enthusiasm. Each of us emerged to a warm round of applause.

Glad though I was to see my parents, my euphoria was tempered with sadness. It was over. The great adventure had ended. Who was I? Where was I going? What next?

∽

Almost a quarter of a century after this story's end, I am sitting in my old friend Gen's living room at her home in New Brunswick. My daughter, attending a summer science program for gifted students at St. Andrews by-the-Sea, is with us for the weekend. Gen and I reminisce about life at HQ CRU.

"Whatever happened to that nice officer cadet you were going out with when I first came down to 47 Company?" she asks.

"That was Trev, the kindest, most caring man I met overseas. We thought the world of each other, but neither of us ever forgot that he had a wife back home. I didn't realize just how much I cared about Trev until after he'd left. I couldn't get him out of my mind. I've often wondered about him. He must have died in battle, probably early in 1945, otherwise he'd have written to me. I tried to find out, then and later, after I got home, but no luck."

"And what about that officer you saw from time to time? I

remember Boxing Day especially. I was heading for the sergeants' mess with a couple of other girls. They were green with envy, watching you and Millie trotting off down the road with those two good-looking guys."

"Ken was my first boyfriend. We'd broken up back home, but we stayed good friends all the time we were in the U.K. Just good friends. Until he was wounded. That changed him. I got a real shock after he'd been wounded in Normandy, when he went into a jealous snit because I mentioned dating someone else."

"Millie told me something about that. She said you were very upset."

"I was. Just two or three weeks before VE Day Ken was wounded again, this time critically. I think that's when he realized how much I meant to him. But of course I didn't even know he'd been wounded a second time until I got a letter he dictated to a nurse in late July. He was still too ill to write himself."

"And by then you were dating Reggie."

"Yes, but I did answer the letter and promised to see Ken after I got home, so that we could have what he called 'a heart-to-heart talk.' But all sorts of unexpected things happened and I didn't get to the hospital until October, and then I was wearing my engagement ring. His mother happened to be there. I didn't stay long."

"What happened to Ken after that? Did you hear later?"

"An old school friend told me he'd recovered well, graduated from UBC, got himself a good job in government. That's all I know, except for a picture my mother sent me, cut out of the Vancouver Sun. Ken and his attractive bride. Sometime in 1949 or '50, perhaps. So he did okay."

"You must have felt conflicted back in that summer, 1945 I mean. Ken and Reggie."

"Not really. I was absolutely besotted with Reggie." I pause. "You were older than me, older and wiser," I tell her, "but I didn't listen to you."

"I had inside information," she says. "Remember Bill, the staff sergeant with the pot belly? I used to chat with him in the sergeants' mess after dinner. He was mess administrator and he knew those men very well. Do you sometimes wish you had listened?"

I look across the room at my lovely seventeen-year-old daughter. I think of her two brothers: clever, handsome teenagers. Great kids all, dearer to me than anything in the world. How could I regret my children?

"No, not at all."

Regret can become at best useless, at worst highly destructive. Each time you come to a crossroad in life, you decide which way to turn. At the time it seems like a free choice, but when you look back, you realize that, given the kind of person you were at that time, with the information then at your disposal, and all the factors acting upon you, you couldn't have done anything else. Despite the wisdom of this, you can easily fall into the "if only" trap. If only you had taken the other road. But then you wouldn't have had all these great experiences. As the journey continues, you become more and more adept at avoiding the "if only" trap. And so I look back upon the past without regret. What happened, happened. That's life!

NOTES

PREFACE (pp. vii–xiii)

1. Dr. Mawdsley was my English teacher at King Edward High School in my senior matriculation year, 1939–1940. We both arrived at the University of British Columbia in September 1940, she to become Dean of Women, with a cross appointment to the English Department as assistant professor, I as a sophomore. At UBC I often dropped into her office for a comforting chat. She was on my side.

CHAPTER ONE: FROM STUDENT TO SOLDIER (pp. 1–15)

1. At that time in B.C., high school senior matriculation was the equivalent of first-year university. I took senior matriculation at King Edward High School because it was cheaper than university, costing $100 as opposed to the university fee of $175. (A $75 difference does not sound like much today, but at that time my father's annual salary as an accountant was $1,800.) Thus my first

year on the UBC campus was actually my second year of university coursework. It was thanks to my German professor at King Edward that I ended up having all of second year's and two-thirds of third year's tuition paid for me. He had recommended me to his wife, a member of the Philanthropic Educational Organization (PEO) Sisterhood, an organization then as now dedicated to assisting promising young women with their education. All I had to do was pass muster at a tea given by a chapter of this society and maintain high grades. I owe much to those generous women.

2. Sometime during the '80s when visiting friends on the West Coast, I came across Dr. Mawdsley's name in the telephone book and called her. We reminisced about our respective problems with UBC's English Department so many years before. "Doris," she said, "the situation was much worse than you realized. Not only were the classes segregated, but also the senior professors set the exams and would not let us juniors know what was on them. They coached their students with those exams in mind. And so of course the men did better." Small wonder that I barely made first-class honours, despite the fact that English had always been my best subject.

3. Pierre became one of the most prolific writers Canada has ever known, with a total of at least sixty books to his credit. He also achieved fame as a newspaper and magazine editor, war correspondent, and television personality. Despite his celebrity status, he never became too big for his boots. Many years after our brief association at UBC, I watched a documentary on TV depicting his life and family and was moved to write a note telling him how much I had enjoyed seeing them all. Knowing how busy he was at that time, I didn't expect a reply. I was surprised and delighted to receive one by return mail. "Of course, I remember you," he wrote. "Janet and I remember you very well." And then he went on to tell

me about various people we both had known and relate a couple of amusing anecdotes. He was a thoroughly genuine person.

4. Frederic Gordon Campbell Wood (1887–1976), born in Victoria, B.C., was educated at McGill and Harvard. He joined the Department of English faculty at the newly created University of British Columbia, where he taught for more than thirty-five years. The Frederic Wood Theatre commemorates his major contributions to theatre in the province.

5. Not until I recently tracked down a book by Lee Stewart titled *It's Up to You*, subtitled *Women at UBC in the Early Years* (UBC Press for the UBC Academic Women's Association, 1990), did I recall how Freddy Wood beat us to the punch, so far as the retraction went. He tried to weasel out of the situation by telling the *Ubyssey* that when he saw us in his class, he thought we were "visitors." He said that for years English 2 (second-year English) had been segregated, but any girls "who had a legitimate reason for being there," i.e., the ten girls who had a course conflict, would be permitted to attend the men's class. He made no mention of the fact that prior to our invasion of his sacred precinct he had already told those ten girls they would *not* be allowed to attend. We were all there protesting a rejection that had already taken place, and he knew it. He was simply trying to save face.

 According to *It's Up to You*, ours was the first student challenge to the English Department's segregation policy. It didn't change things right away, but it was a first step, and it did solve the problem for the ten girls who otherwise would have had to miss one lecture a week in English 2. A few years ago, when my part in the story came to the attention of Martha Piper, first woman president of UBC, she kindly sent me a letter of thanks. I didn't accomplish a great deal back in 1941, but at least I tried.

At that time, I didn't know that the same deplorable discrimination existed also in the Math Department. The men were taught by Dean Walter Gage and senior professors, the women by the juniors. What was the dean's excuse? I wonder. I've never considered math a sexy subject. Surely it does not involve "certain things…that simply cannot be taught in mixed classes"? Well, maybe the "Belle" curve?

6. "A block of regimental numbers was established to be allotted to volunteers as they enlisted. The numbers in blocks of 1,000 preceded by the letter W were coded to the military district in which enlistment transpired, making it easy to discern that W1000 came from District 1 while Military District 12 had obviously recruited W12000." W. Hugh Conrod, *Athene, Goddess of War: The Canadian Women's Army Corps—Their Story* (Consumer and Corporate Affairs, 1983, p. 36). Thus my own number, W11508, indicates that I was the 509th woman to enlist in Military District 11, W11000 being the first.

7. This was our favourite marching song: "Put On Your Little Khaki Bonnet" (sung to the tune of "Put On Your Old Grey Bonnet"):

   Put on your little khaki bonnet, with the maple leaves upon it
   And we'll march to the centre of the fray,
   And you can tell old Hitler that his hopes are even littler
   Now the CWACs are on their way.

   And when the war is over we'll come back to Colonel Dover
   With a million medals to display,
   And we'll tell tall stories of the way we won our glories
   In an old CWAC's home some day.

8. Conscription for home defence began in April 1941. On November 22, 1944, it was announced that conscripts would be sent overseas, according to Bill 80.

CHAPTER THREE: INTRODUCTION TO LONDON (pp. 20–29)

1. "Draft," as used here, is a military term referring to the selection of persons already in the military service to be sent from one post to another detachment. In Ottawa we girls of 42 Company had been "on draft," i.e. in the process of preparing to go overseas. We were in the "second draft" of CWACs selected for such service. Members of 41 Company, the "first draft," had arrived in England six weeks earlier.

2. The full title, which we never used, was *King's Regulations and Orders for the Canadian Militia*.

3. Except for Ken, an ex-boyfriend from UBC whom I saw often, the only lad from my hometown to call on me was Allan McGill, one of the nicest fellows in my high school class. Someone in his squadron had given him my phone number. I recall a pleasant walk along Oxford Street towards Marble Arch on a summer evening in 1943, but can't remember where we dined or what movie we saw. However, my memory was, and is, better than Allan's. Some forty-six years later at a high school reunion, I saw him again and reminded him of our London date. Alas, he couldn't remember ever having seen me in London. What an impressive date I must have been! Recently Allan redeemed himself by giving me a copy of his memoir, *My Life As I Remember It*, inscribed "To Doris with best wishes, and apologies for my failed memory." I have listed Allan's book under "For Further Reading" on page 198. More than just a war memoir, it includes the story of his distinguished career in Canada's diplomatic service.

CHAPTER FOUR: HOSPITALITY IN ABERDEEN
AND TORQUAY (pp 30–38)

1. The program for the "Russian Ballet" at the Winter Garden Theatre
in Drury Lane is typical. The small print reads: "If a public air-raid
warning is sounded in the course of a performance, the audience
will be notified on the illuminated sign in front of the footlights.
This does not necessarily mean that an air raid will take place, and
we recommend you to remain in the theatre. If, however, you wish
to leave, you are at liberty to do so. All we ask is that, if you feel you
must go, you will depart quietly, and, as far as possible, without
disturbing others. The 'Raiders Passed' signal will also be shown
on the illuminated sign. Should any news of particular interest be
received during a performance it will be announced from the stage
at the end of the succeeding scene or act of the play."

Some notices include directions to the nearest air-raid shelter.
One, more concise, for a performance of the National Symphony
Orchestra at the Royal Albert Hall, tells concert-goers: "In the
event of an Air Raid Warning, the audience will be immediately
informed, and those who wish to do so may take shelter either
in the building or in the trenches in Hyde Park or Kensington
Gardens. The concert will continue."

CHAPTER FIVE: NON-HEROES (pp. 39–48)

1. These were large cards, approximately 11 x 13 inches. In the upper
left corner would be the regimental number of the soldier, followed by name and rank. Below would be the soldier's answers to
certain questions—e.g., "Why did you join the Army?"—together
with next of kin, educational level, work experience, and so on. A
letter and number code, "PULHEMS" would indicate health sta-

tus, each letter standing for one part or aspect of the body, e.g., *H* for heart, *M* for mental (intelligence level), each letter accompanied by a number from 1 to 5, from highest to lowest. Thus a highly intelligent person would be an M1, a person well below average an M4. Presumably an M5 would have been discharged as unsuitable for the service, although a 5 in another category might possibly be acceptable.

However, the Army M Test was made up of a number of sections, some not good measures of intelligence, and so one's total M score could be misleading. Although the card included the breakdown of scores, Selection of Personnel and other officers tended to make decisions based on the total. Gen, the woman given the job I had coveted at HQ CRU, obtained a perfect score on the "mechanical" section, worth a disproportionate number of the total points for the entire test. That section simply required the respondent to identify tools from line drawings. Gen had a great advantage over other women: she had worked in a hardware store for six months prior to enlisting.

2. Ken had alerted me to the "fake pay book" ploy. Pay books contained identification data and trade classification as well as pay records. Some married Canadian soldiers carried two of these small books, one legitimate and one they had acquired illicitly and filled out themselves to indicate "single" status. A guy would then show the fake book to the new girlfriend, later maybe even going so far as to propose marriage. Some English girls fell into this trap. Perhaps some of our girls did as well, but this kind of story spreads fast in the army environment, and when I brought up the subject in barracks one evening, I surprised no one.

3. In those days the word "Negro" did not have the negative connotation it has now taken on. It was the accepted term. The terms

"African-American" and "Black" were not yet in vogue. In this as in other respects, I have tried to use the language of the times throughout the book.

CHAPTER SIX: ARMY BLUNDERS AND AIR RAIDS (pp. 49–54)

1. I had always believed these quarters to be new after we moved in, but according to *Athene,* that was not so. They, like the Chesham Hotel, my first London residence, had been renovated especially for the CWAC.

2. The blunders made by headquarters staff were hardly surprising, considering how rapidly the military machine had been cobbled together. Here were all these former civil servants, teachers, office workers, salespeople and others with absolutely no military and very little supervisory experience suddenly thrown into a situation of tremendous responsibility, for which they had absolutely no training and sometimes little aptitude. The wonder is that it all worked as well as it did.

   Our CWAC company officers were far superior to many of the male officrs we encountered at work. These women were often experienced administrators in some professional or voluntary capacity in civilian life. We admired and respected them. They in turn had our best interests at heart. They would go to bat for us whenever they could.

3. Recently I googled "The Memory Project," where Canadian veterans recount their wartime experiences. I was amazed to read an account by ex-CWAC Lois Johnson of being traumatized by London air raids, particularly by the sound of the Hyde Park ack-acks. Since 43 Company, at Lancaster Gate, was the CWAC company closest to those guns, she could have been stationed there when I was, although I do not recognize the name. She reports being sent

home sick and then being hospitalized for two years because she could not get the sound of those guns out of her head. Was she the girl who failed to elicit my sympathy, I wonder? How smug I was! I wasn't at all brave, just foolhardy and lucky enough to be an incredibly sound sleeper.

CHAPTER SEVEN: CIVILIANS AND THE INTERNATIONAL SCENE (pp. 55–62)

1. In her highly detailed account of her World War II experiences as secretary to various VIPs in the Middle East, the Countess of Ranfurly recounts a conversation with Sir Harold MacMichael, British High Commissioner in Jerusalem. She reports that the Jews with whom she socialized thought he was on the side of the Arabs, while the Arabs, whose company she also enjoyed, were convinced that he was pro-Jew. The countess herself, thoroughly familiar with his dispatches and his files, found him determinedly neutral. On one occasion when she summoned up the courage to ask the commissioner to tell her frankly how he felt about the issue, she reports him as saying, "We are not here to judge.... Just remember that Palestine is a very small country and no one can put a pint into a half-pint pot." Quoted in Hermione Ranfurly, *To War with Whitaker: Wartime Diaries of the Countess of Ranfurly, 1939–45* (Mandarin, 1995, pp. 105–6).

2. Now known as Hotel Russell, but in those days we always called it the Russell Hotel. It was popular with servicemen coming to London on leave.

CHAPTER EIGHT: SETTLING INTO THE
WARTIME ROUTINE (pp. 63–69)

1. The Army lectured its male soldiers on the dangers of venereal disease and the importance of using condoms, while lecturing its female soldiers on the dangers of pregnancy and the importance of abstinence. According to my friend Ken, the lectures given to the men often omitted mention of using condoms to prevent pregnancy.

2. While fear of pregnancy was the major factor keeping most of us on the straight and narrow, there was another one, almost equally compelling: the desire at some not far distant point to marry and have children. Guys didn't marry "fast" girls. They happily had sex with anyone they could seduce, but seldom did they wed those girls. The men wanted virgin brides, girls they'd be proud to take home to Mama. This added to the ridiculous imbalance that kept the majority of single women frustrated and a minority extremely busy during the war. Some must have been close to exhaustion! I bitterly resented this double standard.

CHAPTER TEN: THE BUILD-UP TO D-DAY (pp. 85–94)

1. This appears to be the same hospital to which Anthea Penne's father was later sent. I can quite understand what a comedown it must have been after his previous experience in American military hospitals. The Americans had everything!

2. This was yet another advantage to living in barracks rather than in private lodgings, as the Air Force girls did. It was easier to escape compromising situations. "Hank" was not the only American non-com I met who appeared to have unlimited funds. Were those men black marketeers, or merely talented poker players?

The Canadian guys I dated were much less sexually aggressive than some of the Americans. Our military compatriots treated us with respect. "No" meant "no," even if preceded by a fair amount of "necking." Canada was not without its rogues, but at least ours were relatively well-mannered rogues.

Nor did I encounter sexual harassment at work. I knew that it went on in the civilian world, because my father once talked about an incident where he worked. One of the women clerks had come to him in tears over just such a problem with her (and my dad's) employer. But in the Army I neither experienced nor even heard of such treatment. I am amazed by reports of it in today's military establishments. Our set-up, however, was very different from the current one: we had our own corps and lived in our own barracks—totally apart from the men and under the protection of women officers. Had the male officers we worked with tried any funny business, they would have had those women to contend with. We admired and trusted our CWAC officers and would not have hesitated to seek their help.

CHAPTER ELEVEN: SUMMER FUN,
MILITARY MUDDLES, BUZZ BOMBS (pp. 95–107)

1. Years later Phyllis confessed that the doodlebugs were the main reason she volunteered to go over to the Continent with First Echelon in August 1944. It turned out that she had jumped out of the frying pan into the fire. The conditions under which the girls of First Echelon lived and worked were sometimes merely disconcerting, sometimes terrifying. In the former category were the pit stops when in a truck convoy en route towards the front lines. Periodically, the convoy stopped to let a couple of soldiers in the truck ahead of the girls' vehicle jump out, carrying a long can-

vas sheet attached to two poles. One fellow dug his pole into the ground, the other likewise, the thirty or so feet of canvas stretched between the two. Then as the men returned to the truck, the girls ran out and did their business behind the canvas. You had to be able to go on cue. Lacking the kind of innards that make such a feat possible, I stopped envying Phyllis her continental experience right then and there.

Terrifying experiences occurred at times when a sudden change of direction in the fighting put the girls uncomfortably close to the front. At one time, near Antwerp, they risked being almost surrounded by the enemy. One Friday afternoon, they asked the sergeant major for time off to go over to the canteen across the road. She refused, said she wanted some more work done on the files. That was fortunate. A shell landed on the canteen and blew it to smithereens. The blast sent Phyllis across the office into a wall, injuring her knee, but at least she and the rest of the girls survived.

2. Glenn Miller was a greatly beloved American composer and big-band leader whose music has continued to enjoy popularity to this day. Everyone was much saddened when he was declared missing in action just before Christmas 1944. At that time a major in the United States Army Air Force, he was on his way to France to entertain the troops when his plane disappeared in bad weather over the English Channel. No trace of the plane or its occupants was ever found. His status remains "missing in action."

3. Difficult though this may be for some male readers to understand, we girls were not eager for sex. Romance, yes. We had been brought up on the Prince Charming myth and had not yet discovered it to be just that, a myth. And then there were a few girls, two of my friends among them, who avoided dating altogether. Although neither lesbian nor lacking in attractiveness, they spent

their time with the other girls or, on occasion, would go to some function or other as part of a mixed group. They got along well enough with the men they worked with and seemed at ease with them, but never accepted a date. After war ended, both my friends went on to live long and apparently satisfactory lives. One is still going strong. She will no doubt live to be one hundred or more, *virgo intacta.*

CHAPTER TWELVE: FLYING HATS AND FABULOUS COFFEE (pp. 108–115)

1. Battledress (see inset photo section) consisted of roomy pants and a jacket with concealed buttons, rather like a tunic, that I would pull on over my head.

CHAPTER THIRTEEN: MORE THAN ONE KIND OF WOUND (pp. 116–127)

1. I paid the rent in the form of chocolate bars. Sometime in 1943 we had begun receiving a "sweet ration," consisting of two small bars, one Hershey's and one Mars. The ration was irregular, probably averaging once every couple of months. By the time it arrived, I was usually so desperate for something sweet that I ate both bars within a day or two, but by the end of 1943, Ken had somehow acquired an extra dozen, which he passed on to me. The owner of the gown was only too happy to accept this form of payment.

CHAPTER FOURTEEN: WINTER CHILLS (pp. 128–135)

1. The CWAC unit of *The Canadian Army Show* was organized in the fall of 1942 and went on its first national tour in the spring of 1943. CWACs with singing and/or dancing talent were invited to audi-

tion. *The Army Show* included both male and female performers, entertaining the troops on the Continent, often not far from the front lines, as well as in the U.K. In Canada its primary purpose may have been to aid in recruitment. In 1944, an *Army Show* reinforcement unit was located near Farnborough. One evening two of my CWAC friends and I attended a dance there, in response to an invitation from Marcel, a male performer who had transferred to that unit from our Selection of Personnel Office. Alas, for the first and last time in our army experience, my friends and I were wallflowers! The number of men and women present was about even, and the men showed not the slightest interest in us outsiders. Well, Marcel did dance with each of us a couple of times, but only to fulfill his obligation as host.

2. The *News of the World* was the highlight of Sunday mornings in the sergeants' mess. There were always two or three copies on hand. We would hover anxiously over the readers, waiting to swoop down on the paper like vultures, directly anyone showed signs of putting it down. Although today we might find those "news items" tame, the stories were the most scandalous we had ever seen in a newspaper. Not only scandalous but also hilarious, told with a sardonic kind of humour. We especially enjoyed the way they targeted aristocrats. The British class system both intrigued and dismayed us "colonials." However, U.K. citizens appeared to love the *News of the World* as much as we did.

3. Looking at a picture on my wall featuring the entire group of NCOs at HQ CRU, today those men don't look that bad. (At twenty-three, I must have considered any man over thirty "old" and any man over forty "horribly" so!) I now have grandsons the age of some of them. It's all a matter of perspective.

4. Under tremendous pressure to replace the increasing number of

casualties, in November Prime Minister Mackenzie King had agreed to a one-time levy of 17,000 of these men for overseas service. Reportedly, however, only 2,400 reached the front lines.

5. "Right Wheel" is a right turn made while in the process of marching; the whole formation swings around, like the skaters' whip in slow motion.

CHAPTER SEVENTEEN: THE GOLDEN SUMMER (pp. 159–173)

1. In those days no one knew anything about post-traumatic stress disorder (PTSD). It did not become a recognized disorder until the Vietnam veterans lobbied to have it recognized in the 1970s. While the soldier who showed such obvious signs of mental aberration may have received a disability pension on discharge, a pension was typically linked to physical disabilities, not to psychological disorder. Others with less evident symptoms did not get pensions.

It would be almost sixty years before Dr. Lynne Beal, a Toronto psychologist, would come to research the extent of post-traumatic stress disorder among Canadian soldiers who fought at Dieppe, some of whom were captured and incarcerated. The daughter of a Dieppe veteran who had spent almost three years as a POW, Dr. Beal hypothesized that many of these combat veterans and former prisoners of war had post-traumatic stress disorder that had gone undiagnosed and untreated. Her fifty-year follow-up study examined the incidence of PTSD in both groups. Her study showed a high incidence of PTSD in the combat troops and an even higher incidence among those veterans who were also POWs.

Hearings of the Senate Subcommittee on Veterans Affairs received Dr. Beal's research, among other evidence. Subsequently, the Canada Pension Act was changed to recognize psychological disorders resulting from trauma during military service as a pensionable disability. It was only then that POWs obtained compensation, and Dr. Beal herself received a much-deserved Commendation award from the Canadian Minister of Veterans Affairs. Since I had been one of Dr. Beal's supervisors during her internship year of supervised practice to become a psychologist, I was especially delighted when I came across the report of her achievement in the *Canadian Journal of Psychology*.

2. The cover picture of me frolicking in the surf at Bournemouth is one of the many photos Jeanne took while overseas. A few years ago, my niece found the tiny original among her father's papers, had it enlarged and framed, and sent it to me as a surprise gift. Because of Jeanne's expertise and her Hasselblad camera, the enlargement is as sharp as the original.

3. In 1944, with all the focus on northern Europe, after D-Day those men felt ignored. They were still fighting their way through Italy, suffering enormous casualties, while all eyes seemed elsewhere. The plight of these forgotten heroes was given expression in "We Are the D-Day Dodgers," sung to the tune of the popular "Lili Marlene." Several versions can be found on YouTube.

4. This was a smart move. Reggie's heavy army boots would have made swimming very difficult. I wonder how many World War II soldiers drowned, weighed down by their army boots.

5. At the age of fourteen, I learned the proper technique of lying from Mr. Morrow, my high school principal. Mistaking my shyness for duplicity, he told me he knew I was lying because I never looked him in the eye. He had a tiny spot high up on the bridge of his nose. From that moment on, whenever I encountered the man, I forced myself to stare fixedly at that spot, trying hard not to blink. Four years later, when I was leaving the school, Mr. Morrow praised me for having decided honesty was the best policy. "I know you are

telling the truth now," he said. "You always look me in the eye." It was a lesson that came in useful during my military career, especially in protecting me from con artists who might also have perfected this technique. I was less likely to be deceived by them.

6. You could always find several copies of the latest daily newspaper lying around in the sergeants' mess, but few of us kept up with the news. Reading about the war was often depressing, and we never knew what was fact and what was propaganda. In London, however, I had kept abreast of things by visiting the ubiquitous news cinemas. These, or "newsreel theatres," as they were called in New York, had been operating for some time, but I had never heard of them in Canada. The films went on continuously all day and into the evening, featuring the latest news films. You could drop in for an hour or even a half-hour and catch up on current events. It was very convenient when you were waiting for someone or had time to kill between appointments, even when you only wanted to get in out of the rain.

FOR FURTHER READING

Andrews, Allen. *Brave Soldiers, Proud Regiments.* Vancouver: Ronsdale, 1997.

Conrod, W. Hugh. *Athene, Goddess of War: The Canadian Women's Army Corps—Their Story.* [Printed by Wm. Mcnab & Sons, Halifax.] Consumer and Corporate Affairs, 1983.

Day, Frances Martin, Phyllis Spence and Barbara Ladouceur eds. *Memoirs of the Canadian Red Cross Corps.* Vancouver: Ronsdale, 1998.

Johnson, Lois. "Lois Johnson." The Memory Project. [National archives project, an initiative of the Historica-Dominion Institute.] http://www.thememoryproject.com/stories/1471:lois-johnson/.

Maitland, Beatrice McMillan. *Put On Your Tin Helmet and I'll Tell You Some War Stories.* [Published by the author.] Calgary, 2004.

McGill, Allan S. *My Life as I Remember It.* Vancouver: Granville Island Publishing, 2004.

Penne, Anthea. *Old Stones: The Biography of a Family.* Victoria, B.C.: TouchWood Editions, 2010.

Pennefather-McConnell, Nano. *We Never Stopped Dancing: An Airwoman's Scrapbook.* Shawville, Que.: Life Profiles, 2002.

Ranfurly, Hermione. *To War with Whitaker: Wartime Diaries of the Countess of Ranfurly, 1939–45.* Mandarin, 1995.

Russell, Ruth. *Proudly She Marched: Training Canada's World War II Women in Waterloo County. Vol. 1 of Canadian Women's Army Corps.* Kitchener-Waterloo, Ont.: Canadian Federation of University Women, 2006.

Stafford, David. *Ten Days to D-Day: Citizens and Soldiers on the Eve of the Invasion.* Boston: Da Capo Press, 2005.

Stewart, Lee. *It's Up to You: Women at UBC in the Early Years.* Vancouver: UBC Press for the UBC Academic Women's Association, 1990.

ABOUT THE AUTHOR

Doris Gregory was born Doris Filmer-Bennett in Vancouver, B.C., a city she still considers the most beautiful in the world, leaving it in 1942 to embark on the great adventure recounted in this book. In 1946 she resumed study at the University of British Columbia. Two years later she accepted a fellowship at the University of Minnesota, then taught briefly at the University of New Hampshire before staying at home eleven years to care for her three children. Subsequently, she worked as a school psychologist in Ontario. Later, when her interest turned to clinical psychology, particularly family therapy and the treatment of anxiety disorders, Doris undertook extensive study at the Clarke Institute of Psychiatry in Toronto before opening an independent clinical practice, publicized by her weekly newspaper column, "Life Psycle."

In retirement, Doris fulfilled her dream of returning to her beloved Vancouver. During working years she had travelled through Europe with her children and attended conventions in the USA, Britain, and Australia. She has since enjoyed longer stays abroad, including vacations in Bermuda and the South Pacific, as well as the pursuit of language studies in northern Quebec, Mexico, and Guatemala. Now she keeps busy with writing and exercise classes, volunteer activities, time with family, and socializing with dear friends old and new. She finds every day a delight.

INDEX

Citations of photographs are in bold

43 Company, 93, 99, 106,
107, 123, 137, 188
47 Company, 93, 97, 100,
102, 10**8**, 112, 134–35,
163, 178
Orderly Office, 98, 106
ack-acks, *see* anti aircraft
guns
Air Force High Command,
28
air raids, 33, 49, 51, 65, 68,
87, 93, 188
shelters for, 2, 186
wardens of, 29, 54, 69
Aldershot, 44, 95, 126, 132,
166

American Negro Regiment,
47
anti-aircraft guns, 1–2, 53,
188
Army Show, 129
Athene, 107, 184, 188
Away Without Leave (AWL),
93, 105
barracks, 8, 10, 27–28, 47,
66, 68, 79, 85, 92, 97, 106,
109, 119, 121, 190–91
Stanhope Terrace, 50, 63,
69
Argyle, 14
Chesham Hotel, 21–22,
51, 188

basic training, 111
Basingstoke Canal, 99, 103
BBC, 76
Beck, Andy (pay sergeant), 130, 136–37, 172
Belfast, 137, 139, 152, 155
    Grand Central Hotel, 156–57
Bennett, R.B., 76
Berton, Pierre, 5–7, 182
Big Ben, 23
blackouts, 29, 65, 82, 94,
Brackman-Kerr Milling Company, 32
Britton, Sir Harry, 76,
Broadlands, 81–82
Brown, Captain, 49, 77, 88
Buckingham Palace, 50
buzz bombs, *see* pilotless planes
Cambridge, 70, 72
Canada House, *see* Canadian Military Headquarters
Canadian Military Headquarters (CMHQ), 23, 47, 52, 128, 133–34
Canadian Scottish Regiment, 25
Canadian University Press (CUP), 7

Canadian Women's Army Corps (CWAC), 4, 7, 9, 13, 16, 21, 59, 64–65, 76, 87, 100, 107, 132, 156, 160, 163, 177–78, 184, 188, 193–94
    officers, 104, 112, 123–24, 134, 191
    regulations, 10, 27, 98, 105, 134–36
    reinforcements, 133, 185
    socializing, 29, 40–41, 83–84, 93, 101, 126, 130
Christmastime overseas, 22, 44, 85, 124, **125**, 126–27
civilian life
    hesitance to return to, 160–61
clerks, 13, 108, 112, 171
conscription, 12, 185
Cornwall, 35, 37, 88, 90, 121
Court of Inquiry, 52
Cripps, Lady Isobel, 31
Cripps, Sir Stafford, 31
dating, 40–41, 43, 78, 92, 94, 99, 118, 126, 134
    married soldiers, 87, 105-6, 131, 162
Davy belt harness, 22, 51

D-Day, 46, 96, 162, 190, 196, 199
Depression, the, 43
doodlebugs, *see* pilotless planes
Dover, 161
Dublin, 143-50, **148**, 152, **157**
    Shelbourne Hotel, 146, **147**
Dundalk, 137, 139–43, 152
educational leave, 80–81, 100–1, **102**
Éire, 136-37, 139–42, 144, 146–147, 151–152, 154
English Civil War, 72
Falmouth, 121–22
Ferguson, Major (psychologist), 39, 91
First Canadian Division, 44
Free French forces, 47, 52
Gestapo, 46–47
Gough, Captain, 98, 107
Grant Square, 96, 106, 109, 134
Grantchester, 74
Halifax, 15, 173, 175
Headquarters, Canadian Reinforcement Units (HQ CRU), 99, 117, 130, 133, 136, 162, 178, 187, 194

HMS *Victory* (ship), 113
homecoming greetings, **175**, 176–77
hospital, *see* infirmary
Hyde Park, 50, 52–53, 186, 188
identity discs, 100
infirmary, 74, 76–79, 83, 88–89, 117–18, 160, 170
    enemy hospitals for POWs, 46–47
International Club, 59–60
Irish Sea, 20, 138, 157
Italy, 162, 164–67
Kennedy, Col. Joan, 10
King Arthur's castle, 90
Kings Regulations Canadian (KR Can), 24
Kingston Penitentiary (KP), 43
kit inspection, 14, 97–98
K-rations, see rationing
Lancaster Gate, 50, 188
Leicester Square, 33, 58
Line, Colonel, 96
London, 1, 20–21, **26**, 29, 31–32, **33**, **34**, 46, **60**, **75**, 91, **120**, 197
    Blitz, 10, 21, 23, 28, 169
    High Command, 51

Malta, 29

Mawdsley, Dr. Dorothy, 5,
181–82

McPherson, Misses, 30–32

medical records, 47, 77, 98

Millie, Sergeant Major, 107,
111, 123, 126, 179

Military District 11 (MD 11),
7, 14, 184

Mountbatten, Lady Edwina,
81–83

Mountbatten, Patricia, 81

Navy
Merchant, 61–62
British, 83–84

New Forest, 81

Newry, 137, 139, 153–56

News of the World, 130

Nieuw Amsterdam (ship), 174-
176, **176**

Non-Commissioned Officers
(NCOs), 21, 28, 41, 101,
124, 130, 159, 194

Normandy, 46, 161, 179

Old Stones, 46

Oxford, 33, 70, 72, 168, 185

Pankhurst, Emmeline
(suffragette), 57

Parliament Buildings, 23

Penne, Anthea, 46, 190

Pennefather-McConnell,
Nano, 46, 105–6, 158, 199

Pethick, Frederick, 57–58

Pethick-Lawrence, Mrs.
Emmeline, 56–58

Piccadilly Circus, 33

pilotless planes vii, 95, 97,
99–100, 191

Plymouth, 35–37

Portsmouth, 81, 112

pregnancy, 44, 65, 104–5,
107

Princes Street, 71, 104

Prisoners of War (POWs),
46, 59, 163, 195

promotion, 52, 110, 112

pyjama parade, *see* pregnancy

Q-(qualification) Cards, 40

Queen Elizabeth (ship),
15–16, **17**, **18**, 19, 72, 84,
138

Queens University, 7

rationing, 20, **28**, **31**, 38, **41**,
82–83, 126

Records Building, 40–41

Red Cross, 85, 198

reinforcements to the
Continent, 116, 128,
132–33

Royal Canadian Air Force
   Women's Division
   (RCAF WD), 27
Royal Family, **11**, 15, 50–51,
   169–70
Russell Hotel, 61, 189
Scotland, 20, 32, 103
Selection of Personnel,
   40–41, 91, 93, 96, 112,
   125, 130, 133, 171, 187, 194
Shakespeare, 34, 71, 101
Southampton, 81, 85, 112
   School of Navigation in,
   80, 85
Spam, 75
Stars and Stripes, 8
stenographers (stenos), 11,
   13, 23, 42
Stratford-upon-Avon, 70–72,
   73
Surrey, 45, 70, 74
Sussex Square, 50
Toronto, 8, 96, 167, 173, 177
Torquay, 31, 33, 35–36, 38,
   186
Trafalgar Square, 23
U-boats (German), 3, 19, 165
Ubyssey, 4–5, 7, 183
Ulster, 155–56

Underground (transporta-
   tion), 28, 49, 94, 97, 168
uniforms, 8–11, 14–15, 27,
   111–12
University of Aberdeen, 31
University of British
   Columbia (UBC), 55–56,
   87, 161, 167, 179, 181, 185,
   199
   gender discrimination at,
   4–6, 57, 182–83
U.S. Army Negro Chorus, **86**
V-1s & V-2s, *see* pilotless
   planes
Vancouver, 7–8, 14, 22, 32,
   72, 78–79, 161, 168, 173,
   177–179, 198–201
Vancouver Sun, 78, **79**, 179
VE Day, 111, 159–60, 170, 179
Veterans Affairs, 161
VJ Day, 169–79
wages, **9**, 35, 67, 79, 87, 130,
   136, 172, 187
Walter Scott Monument, 71,
   104
Well of St. Keyne, 37
Westminster Abbey, 23
Women's Army Corps
   (WAC), 7, 16, 67, 81, 156,
   181, 184, 198–99

Wood, Professor Frederic, 5, 6, 183

Work Point base (Victoria), 8–9

World Unity Society, 58

World War I, 56, 74

YWCA hostel, 99

zombie (derogatory), *see* conscription